Rodeo Queen 101

ANNE T. REASON

Brains and Beauty

Brains and Beauty
Responsible and a sense of duty
Hair that glistens in the sun,
Hands callused from work that must be done.
Educating, lecturing, and travel
Whether in a suit or in a saddle,
She is articulate and poised
And never is ruffled by the boys.
She can do any job a man can do
In old Wranglers or in a sparkly crown of
silver And blue
She is a Lady at all times,
No one is ever so fine,
For she is found
With her boots on the ground,
A cowgirl and a Rodeo Queen with a
sparkling Crown !

By: Anne T. Reason

Printed in the United States of America

LCCN: 2020916932
ISBN: Softcover   978-1-64908-306-7
           eBook   978-1-64908-305-0

Republished by: PageTurner Press and Media LLC
Publication Date: 09/11/2020

To order copies of this book, contact:

PageTurner Press and Media
Phone: 1-888-447-9651
order@pageturner.us
www.pageturner.us

Dedication

To my husband, Dick Reason

I am most pleased to say that he has been a farmer/ rancher, rodeo contestant in saddle bronc and bareback bronc riding. He has also been a trauma nurse, a farrier, a wrangler, and a western movie extra. Now retired, he does whatever needs to be done at a rodeo. He also judges rodeo queen competitions, local, home town competitions, rodeo circuit competitions, and as a member of Miss Rodeo America, Inc. he judges state competitions.

He is my teacher, mentor and my best friend.

Acknowledgements

I am most grateful to all of the contributors to this book. Most are friends and instantly said "yes, I would be most happy to help", without any thought of financial compensation. They are true friends and true believers in rodeo and the rodeo queen program.

They are: Zona Vig, editor, South Dakota; Wilma Fulgum, editor, New Mexico; Dona Ruthaford, editor & Rodeo Queen Director, New Mexico; Bob Hays, Rodeo Royalty Judge, Arizona; Dick Reason, Rodeo Royalty judge, Arizona; Tiffany Leo, Rodeo Queen Director, Arizona; Carol Richardson DVM, Arizona; Robert J. Rose DC, Arizona; Terry Rose, Cosmetics, Arizona; Nancy Head, Rodeo Royalty Mom, Arizona; Katie Hill, Miss Rodeo Arizona 2007, California; Marjon Brady Brown, Miss Rodeo USA 2000, Arizona; Brandy Dejon, Miss Rodeo America 2000, California; Kayla Sperlock Duba, Miss Rodeo California 2005, Texas; Honeycutt Rodeo inc., Colorado; Karen Womack Vold, Rodeo Queen & wife of stock contractor Harry Vold, Colorado; Kari Puriton, Rodeo Queen Contestant, Wyoming; Bronc Rumford, Past President of Miss Rodeo America & stock contractor, Kansas; Jim Fain, rodeo photographer, Utah.

A special note of gratitude goes to Nancy Head. Because of my post- polio syndrome, she offered to do all the typing and the research for the glossary. As a past novice rodeo queen "mum" she offered invaluable information as to how lost she was the first time her daughter ran for a rodeo royalty title. She learned to ask lots of questions and wished there had been a guidebook for rodeo queen and teen queen moms. I have heard so many novice rodeo royalty moms say "Oh, if only I knew what was ahead of us, maybe we both might have been better prepared. We need a guide book."

It was Nancy Head who brought this to my attention and that I should write this book. With her help, even though we live 300 miles apart, this book became possible. I call her my friend and collaborator.

Table of Contents

> "A man has to blaze his own trail. Mine was to the west."
>
> **Jubel Sackett by Louis L'Amour**

Introduction

Hey, you actually picked up the book. This is your lucky day because this book is really a good read. Wait, don't put this book down. I know, I know, the title sounds like you are enrolling in school again. However, if you have a daughter, like the one on the cover of this book,(and wasn't it the cover that caught your eye?) she might say to you, sooner or later, that she wants to be a rodeo queen.

Hang on, this is not a dull, dry book. This is a book about being a first time queen or teen queen. It is also helpful for the queen "mum" as she takes on her roles as secretary, chauffeur, "Lady in Waiting" and most of all, confidant. "Oh my, this is going to be a lot of work and I already have so much to do." Yup, a very true thought. Most of us, however, consider the growth and polish that you and your daughter will develop and how this will give her more self-confidence. This experience will help her throughout her life.

Don't forget the fun. Yes, I said fun: selecting all of the beautiful clothing together, getting in shape together, running, exercising, lifting weights, and even eating a healthy diet. Yuck! You'll be amazed at all the different combinations you can come up with for chicken and salads. But most of all, is the quality time the two of you will share while working on health and endurance and the inevitable personal conversations that will happen during the drives to rodeos. I think of this book as a combination of the yellow pages phone book, a research library, and a dictionary. I call it "yellow relibtionary". This is my book, so I have the privilege of making up my own words.

This is a how-to-find-something book, with answers for rodeo queens and rodeo queen moms. Oh, I almost forgot, this endeavor will include the whole family and a few friends. This is unlike anything you have ever done. How do I know this? Well, I have been around rodeo most of my life. Sometimes, I even had to sneak out of my folks' house to watch cowboys train horses. I'll make a deal with you. Read the introduction first, then the table of contents. If you still think you don't need this book, okay. But at least you now have an inkling of what lies ahead of you.

You will also know that this book is written by knowledgeable, practical, experienced people in rodeo, such as rodeo queen contestants, rodeo queen judges, title holders, successful coaches,

equine veterinarians, rodeo queen directors, and most of all, queen mothers, who have learned by trial and error and by asking tons of questions. This book is designed to hopefully eliminate some of the frustrations, confusions, and stresses you will face over the next year or so, by minimizing some of the problems mentioned above. This will enable you to have a wonderful and exciting year and, if you choose, to go on to other titles. Keep this book handy at all times, because as you progress to circuit and state competitions, much of this information will still apply.

My name is on the cover of the book, Anne T. Reason, not because I am so great, but because I am an observer. I try to listen to those who are experts in their fields, and I have a big mouth. I am not afraid to ask questions, and neither should you. I have never competed in rodeo as a rodeo queen contestant because I contracted polio in 1954, one year before the vaccine. However, I still grew up with an undying passion for rodeo.

Here is a thumbnail sketch of my background. In Yuma, Arizona, when I was a child, it was a small farm and ranch town. Our Rodeo, is called the Silver Spur Rodeo (single spur). It was a big social event. Each day the town honored the different groups of people who truly made up the Arizona culture. For example: Europeans, Native Americans, Mexicans, Asians, the Buffalo Soldiers, the military, River Men, ranchers, cowboys, farmers, and, of course, the old sheriff. I guess looking back, it was a small snapshot of America.

I grew up with the wonderful cacophony of melodic sounds of different English accents and languages. Rodeo was a truly uniting event, very much a part of our Arizona culture and American history.

Arizona has the legal bragging rights of having the world's oldest rodeo and the world's oldest continuous rodeo: Prescott and Payson, respectively. We also have the bragging rights of having more team ropers than any other state. You would never guess that I am proud of Arizona. My background is in fine arts and helping to raise money through sponsorship to support the arts. However, my heart has always been in our western heritage. There are rodeos held in all 50 states. It is becoming very popular in several European countries. And why not, this Country is made up of all the people of the world. At the age of four, I fell in love with the classic event in rodeo, saddle bronc riding. Years later, I met and married a saddle bronc rider, who at the age of 52, even though his knees were shot and he had arthritis in his neck, rode his first bull. Rodeo gets in your blood and you just can't shake it.

When I first married Dick, I thought I knew everything about rodeo. BOY WAS I WRONG! The first couple of years I asked lots of questions. I know I drove him nuts. I began to learn more about the people in rodeo, like the contestants, rodeo secretaries, judges, timers, chute bosses, stock contractors, committee members, announcers, sound personnel, bull fighters, clowns, barrelmen, truck drivers, veterinarians, photographers, wranglers, and rodeo sponsors. I asked tons of questions of these people. I told you I have a big mouth; almost as big as my curiosity. As I began to learn the true culture of rodeo, I developed an even greater passion for the sport, the people, their duties, responsibilities, and most of all, THEIR DEEP LOVE AND APPRECIATION FOR THEIR LIVESTOCK.

Somehow, I forgot to speak to rodeo queens. Coming from a classical theater background, I knew several celebrities from moves and television, so asking a rodeo queen for her picture and autograph was nothing special for me. They were just another celebrity.

My husband Dick and I became active in the Turquoise Circuit, which includes both New Mexico and Arizona, and is part of the (PRCA) circuit program. Yet again another educational process started. It seems in rodeo you are constantly learning new things. After a few years, we became sponsors to help support our circuit.

Because of our involvement in our circuit, I was asked to submit my resume to become a member of the board of directors for Miss Rodeo Arizona. What an eye opener! I started the process of educating myself in a whole different arena of rodeo. I also found that my background in fine arts and theater came in very handy, so don't say you can't be involved in rodeo because you are an accountant or a school teacher. You will be amazed at what you do know and what you have to offer. In college, I learned one thing that I could apply to daily living: You don't need to know everything, you just need to know where to find the information. I hope this book fills that need.

"All things are possible to him that believeth."

Mark 9:23

Chapter 1

Rodeo Queen 101

Why is this book so important, you might ask? "I am intelligent, I can learn as I go." Well, just read on. It's not fun to go into a new area without some knowledge. If my daughter had come into the kitchen and said "Hi Mom, I want to be a rodeo queen," I think I would have dropped the glass I just cleaned right onto the floor. This is the time that we need to be calm and to take a deep breath and say, "Oh that might be fun!" Dry your hands and ask your daughter to join you at the kitchen table or wherever the two of you can be most comfortable. Here is what I think I would have said to my daughter. "I think that is a wonderful idea. Why did you decide you want to be a rodeo queen?" <u>Never</u> discourage enthusiasm or

1

ambition in your children. " Oh mom I saw them at the rodeo. They wear beautiful clothes, they get to ride in the arena, and they get to chase cattle. They get to wear a crown and banner and everyone thinks they are gorgeous. They get to sign autographs and pass out their pictures,…" Whoa. Just take a breath. Well, yes they do. That's the fun part of it, but that's not all of it. It's just a little cherry on top of the whipped cream.

Being a rodeo queen is a competition of knowledge. I can't stress this enough! Beauty has absolutely nothing to do with it. It's nice if you're good looking, but it doesn't matter. In a rodeo queen competition, knowledge and personality are the traits you should focus on. And by personality I mean being even. Don't throw a fit, don't be pouty, and always be smiling. Look at people. Say "I'm glad you're at the rodeo." Don't lose your temper or show that you're tired. Keep an even temper and show that you have a tremendous amount of information to impart. Practice with your mother or a friend so that you will never hesitate to elaborate. "I'm so glad you're here at the rodeo, are you having fun? Is this your first rodeo? Do you have any questions about any of the events?" Chat with them, explain to them. You need to know the history of every single event and why it has a purpose. A lot of studying is ahead for you.

To get started, buy a three ring binder and divider sheets with tabs for labeling the different areas of information. Put in lots of lined notebook paper. Label the titles of subjects on the tabs, such as, Sponsorship, Speech, Horsemanship, Impromptu, Rodeo Knowledge, Equine Knowledge, Modeling,

Interview, etc. You will find yourself referring to this notebook often.

Note cards are great for studying. Put questions on one side, and answers on the other. The pockets in the notebook will come in handy to carry the note cards.

You need to study and learn the rules of your rodeo association. You will need to learn about the circuit system that is in the Pro Rodeo Cowboys Association, the PRCA. You will need to learn about the anatomy of the rodeo animals (bulls, steers, calves, horses), and compare them to the anatomy of humans. Talk to your equine and bovine veterinarian. You can contact the PRCA office in Colorado Springs, Colorado, for free information about livestock welfare. You can find this number on the internet. Since I am associated only with the PRCA, I can tell you that they have sixty-three rules to protect the animals. There are not as many rules to protect the contestants, really. If the ground is bad for the animal or the weather is bad, they will stop the rodeo. It doesn't matter about the contestant. They can "turn out" if they want withdraw. The stock contractors and the judges care about the animals. They don't want them hurt. These animals can cost from $1,000.00 to $50,000.00 <u>per</u> animal. Looking at it from a business standpoint, who would harm an investment of that amount? You wouldn't. Looking at it from the cowboy's point of view, you paid to ride that animal, you want it to buck hard, you want it to run hard in the time events, and <u>you appreciate the natural athletic abilities of the animal</u>.

If you don't have a horse, it's pretty hard to run for rodeo queen. Investigate about leasing a horse. How much is that going to cost? Perhaps you could trade work for using a horse, like a barter system in lieu of cash payment. There is so much that has to be addressed in this book as you can obviously see.

Meet with the rodeo queen director and see what she expects her new queen and teen queen to do. See what the responsibilities are and what the committee expects the rodeo royalty to do throughout the year. Ask about the contract and if you can see one. Many committees have a legal contract that you will be signing. If you are under 18, your parent or guardian will sign for you. If there is anything you don't understand, ask the queen director. Don't be shy about asking questions. This is to <u>protect</u> you. Also, get the address and phone number of the past queen and teen queen and go visit with them. See what it was like for them. Talk to their parents and see how much it costs. Find out if they had sponsors who might be willing to sponsor you.

You should go to as many rodeo queen clinics as possible. Every clinic will offer something new. Make sure you keep all of the clinic information in your three ring binder. Keep up to date on current events and who are the top cowboys and cowgirls in your rodeo association.

In the back of this book you will find a glossary of rodeo terms and their meanings. It is really important to study these words.

There are many web sites for studying questions frequently asked of rodeo queens. This will come in handy for the private interviews. There are websites where you can find rodeo queen clothes and designers. Do keep in mind that all web sites are subject to change and new ones always appear. One that is used a lot now is "Rodeo Queen Pageant Clothes".

During the year before the competition, you should travel to one or two of the required rodeos. See how tired you are. Then consider if you are ready to travel another four or five hours to get to a different rodeo. Are you too tired to put on your makeup, do your hair, put on your boots and wranglers, check in, put on your sash and crown, get your horse ready and do all the things necessary to be prepared for the grand entry, and other duties that may be required by the host queen director. Know when to be at the gate for the grand entry.

Let's say that you are the queen and you have decided to attend an out-of-town rodeo. You should contact the host queen director and let her know that you will be attending their rodeo. Ask for any papers you need to fill out in advance. If there is a parade, you will need to fill out those applications well in advance. This is good etiquette.

When you are a rodeo queen, you will need to give your information card to the announcer at least two hours before the rodeo. He has a lot of paperwork and a lot of facts to announce. If there is a lot of information he will need to announce, he may simply say, "This is Suzy Q from Rattlesnake Rodeo." If he has more time, you can put down some of your credits like 4H, gymkhana, junior rodeo, etc.,so he can fill in the time. But, the most important information is your title, your name, and the name of the rodeo you represent. Also, if you have a name that is difficult name to pronounce and/or if your ancestors came from a foreign country, spell out the name phonetically. Even a English name can be hard to pronounce sometimes. Find out if you will be carrying a flag in the grand entry, or carrying a sponsor flag during the rodeo. The director of the grand entry will hand the announcer the list of people in the order they will enter the arena in, the sponsors, the queens, etc., so don't worry about that. It is important that he can read your title, your first and last name properly, and the name of your rodeo.

There might be two rodeos on your schedule to attend on the same weekend. My advice would be to go to the one on Saturday that is the furthest away from home. Then on Sunday go to the second rodeo that is closer to home. When traveling to multiple rodeos on the same weekend, you need to consider fatigue on you and the horse, and the cost of fuel. Let the queen directors know that you will be attending only one performance and which day that will be.

When packing, don't forget to pack healthy snacks, plenty of water and juice to drink. Don't forget the vitamin pills, sunscreen, band aids, etc. Most important, pack your hat, crown, and pins to attach your banner. You need to pack your chaps. Notice the plural? Many rodeo royalty have several pairs of chaps for different outfits, including "tough enough to wear pink" chaps. Talking about chaps, if you are given the opportunity to design your own chaps, keep it simple so they are legible from a distance. You need to count how many blouses and jeans you will need. Tip: try to mix and match to cut down on cost and not to take up too much room. You really need to pack more than one hat and several pairs of boots. Don't forget makeup, curlers, hairspray, clips, bobby pins, tape, and other non-revealing clothes. Making a checklist will help ensure you don't forget anything.

Next you pack what you need for your horse. Make sure there are at least two headstalls, several bits, extra reins, polo wraps, saddle, saddle pads, and two flag boots (you need to practice at home carrying the flag and for your horse to become used to it!). Here is a suggestion: Tie old pillow cases or sheets along the fence line to represent sponsor banners. This way your horse won't be spooked when entering the area. You will also need to carry all meds, feed for the horse, and a water bucket or two.

Okay, back to reality. You are just visiting to see if this is what you really want to do. Talk to other queens and visit with their parents.

See if you will be asked to do any public speaking. How many T.V., radio, and media interviews will have to be done? Will you be required to attend committee meetings and circulate at rodeo socials? Remember, the name "rodeo queen" really means, <u>independently contracted, public relations personnel for a major corporation</u>. Now, try putting that on a crown!

Always remember, if you or your parent complain too much, become demanding, gossipy, be pushy, make unkind or unnecessary remarks about other contestants, rodeo royalty, other moms, the rodeo committee, or rodeo personnel, it will not only give you a bad name and no one will want to work with you, but most of all it will harm your chances to be a successful rodeo queen. I cannot stress this enough -- never gossip. You may think these thoughts. You have every right to think them. <u>Keep bad thoughts to yourself</u>. Never verbalize them. Or your reputation will be damaged for a long time.

The young women who are rodeo royalty have to be on their best behavior at all times. They must show that they are friendly, knowledgeable, and have high moral standards. The same applies to their parents. If you notice an infraction by someone at a rodeo event that you are visiting, tell that queen director. You should also notify your queen director of the infraction, and of the actions that you took to the host rodeo queen director, what her suggestions were, and what her actions were. What did you do about the situation? Did you follow what the host rodeo queen director suggested or did you just do what you thought was best or just let it drop?

Here are thoughts about rodeo royalty, from a friend, **Karen Womack Vold**. She is the wife of a stock contractor, a former rodeo queen, and the first Miss Rodeo Arizona.

> When you have been chosen a winner over others, you have an obligation to be a good example. Young girls with dreams of being a queen look up to you, so you need to be a good role model.
>
> When you are representing your rodeo, town, or state, in queen attire, always conduct yourself properly, whether it's a

TV. or radio interview, giving a speech, somewhere, sitting at a head table at a luncheon or dinner, or at any public function. Good manners and speech are always noticed. Don't drink excessively(non-liquer) and embarrass yourself and who you represent.

<u>Don't be late</u>. Start early and allow enough time for things to go wrong, or get stuck in a traffic jam, etc. Always find out from a rodeo committee source what time their rodeo starts and don't take for granted what you read in the newspaper, as they are not always correct.

Be prepared to ride in parades and grand entries. If you are on your own horse, be sure it is well groomed and able to be controlled in that event. As a stock contractor's wife, I can tell you it is much appreciated when we receive a hand written thank you note from a queen that we have furnished a horse for her to ride, whether it be in a competition, parade, grand entry, or carrying a flag. It is also a smart idea to know how to carry a flag on your horse, in case you are ever asked to do so. Make sure you never lose your hat! Whether it is pinned on with bobby pins or now days they use some kind of adhesive.

In all fairness to you and your horse, if you are ever involved in doing some kind of opening for a rodeo, plan to have a rehearsal. You and your horse need to be familiar with the arena and timing, so the first performance is not a rehearsal.

Plan ahead to take care of details when visiting out-of-town rodeos. Get your proper credentials for getting thru the gate. Don't argue or make a scene with the people on the gate who are only doing their job. It causes hard feelings. They don't know who you are if you aren't in queen attire or wearing a banner, etc. It is not a requirement to have expensive clothing to be a rodeo queen. Good grooming, cleanliness, good conduct, manners, and horsemanship will outweigh an expensive wardrobe.

Personal Note from the author: If there is not a mother in the young lady's life, then a big sister, grandmother, aunt, or cousin will do just fine. Yes, even her dad can help. I have seen many dads learn to do "queen hair," make up, and solicit help from others on clothing. Nothing is impossible if you truly want it. You just have to think outside of the box and BELIEVE.

Also, whenever you read a quote and the word "man" is used, it also means "WOMAN." We are talking about the thought, the meaning of the words, not the gender.

> **"Pass on good advice. That is all it's good for."**
>
> *Savvy Sayings* by Ken Alstad

Chapter 2

Queen Directors and Judges

Rodeo queen directors are the foundation of the whole program. If they make the job a twelve month job, you have a good director and program. The two rodeo queen directors I have selected take their job seriously in every respect. One of the their many duties is selecting good judges. The two I selected are well known for their rodeo knowledge and fairness.

The two rodeo queen directors who are contributing their knowledge here are Tiffany Leo, Andy Devine Days Rodeo Royalty director, from Kingman, Arizona,

11

and Dona Rutherford, the Turquoise Circuit Director from Las Cruces, New Mexico.

The two judges are Bob Hays and Dick Reason. Bob Hays is well known throughout Arizona for his judging abilities for PRCA rodeo queen and high school rodeo queen competitions. Dick Reason has judged rodeo queen competitions throughout Arizona and the southwest. He has also judged in South Dakota and Arkansas. He has judged both PRCA and State Rodeo Associations competitions.

From *Tiffany Leo:*

In preparing young ladies for our local Rodeo Queen Pageant, it starts from the moment they pick up or download the Pageant Application. Included on it are all of the areas of information that they will be expected to know, including websites and publications on where to find the information.

Speech topic is also given at this time and the contestant is encouraged to have their speech done and memorized at this point. Questions on their speech, pointers, ideas, etc. are given if the girls ask but actual speech practices are not something done, to prevent speeches being duplicated.

About six weeks prior to the actual competition date, we start having regular meetings. Once to twice a week we have a horsemanship practice on horseback, where the girls learn the pattern. At these practices they are given the chance to perfect their horsemanship skills, including going over the pattern given, a flag run, a hot lap, and a personal interview. This is to prevent any "surprises" the actual day, and helps the girls feel more confident and relaxed. Rodeo knowledge, PRCA knowledge and cowboy standings, parts of the horse, parts of the riding equipment, general equine knowledge, and current events (including the world, U.S., and locally) is also studied at these practices. Before leaving each practice the contestants are encouraged to practice, practice, practice, before the next meeting the following week. Individual riding lessons and any other help is also set up, if interested, at this time.

Six to eight weeks before we hold a small Queen Clinic where the above mentioned is gone over as well as arena etiquette, rodeo etiquette, proper personal hygiene, rodeo queen hair, make-up, proper dress, a mock interview, speech delivery, modeling, questions that may be asked, and a very thorough information study packet is given. Every contestant walks away knowing everything they need to know to be a winner.

Expectations of the title they are running for is also given during this pre-competition time. All girls and parents are informed of what is expected of them, as individuals and as a family, in the event that they win the title. Community involvement, travel, expense, personal actions, etc. are all communicated.

All of this information puts everyone on an even playing ground. The rest is up to the contestant!!

From *Dona Rutherford:*

When Anne Reason asked me to write about being a rodeo queen director, I wasn't sure what I wanted to say. Director of the Miss Turquoise Circuit Pageant is a job filled with lots of work, loads of fun, and a simple amazement at how wonderful some of our younger generation actually is. Being Vice Chairman of the Miss Rodeo New Mexico Pageant for four years and a member of the national Advisory Council for Miss Rodeo America, has given me a deep insight into the Pageant world and the young women who represent the sport of rodeo around this wonderful land of ours. Some have been prima donnas, others downright hard to work with. As a whole, I wouldn't trade my job for anything in the world!

Just what does the Director do? More importantly, what doesn't she do? There are so many things that must be taken care of to prepare for the Pageant; including booking rooms, finding judges, preparing for the Fashion Show and Coronation, getting awards donated, etc. But after the contest is over, your job is to be the best friend, second Mom, coordinator for events, confessor, and jack of all trades with the young woman who has just won the crown. She may be scared to death and have no idea what she just got herself into; so it's your job to make the transition from contestant to seasoned rodeo queen an easy one for her. It's a big job, but if you have a good girl, it's so much easier.

What do I expect of my girls or any girl wearing a rodeo royalty crown? First and foremost, the young woman wearing the crown of a rodeo queen is expected to be an example for everyone who sees her. She is in the public eye and must portray good sportsmanship, have high moral and ethical character, and reflect careful and humane treatment of animals. Here are some of the things I look for and expect from Miss Turquoise Circuit.

Knowledge – It is very important that she understand the sport of rodeo in its entirety – enough to be able to sell rodeo to anyone and everyone she comes in contact with. This could be someone who walks in off the street who has never seen a rodeo, to a world champion cowboy or cowgirl. She must be able to communicate intelligently, with dignity and showing a sincere interest in our sport. When you have that crown on your hat, you must be self-assured and able to stand in front of a group of people and talk about an upcoming event or just rodeo in general with confidence.

Appearance – I am pretty strict about how MTC appears in public. She is told that when she is traveling, she must always keep in the back of her mind that she may be recognized and therefore she must be dressed appropriately. I don't require her to wear full uniform when traveling, unless she is flying, but she should be dressed in an appropriate manner. No short-shorts or sweat pants; no skin exposed. Always with clean, combed hair, and clean nails. She has to have a private life, but for one year that includes dressing in an appropriate manner every time she leaves her house.

At official appearances I do not recommend low rise jeans, either in a contest or after being crowned. They are not flattering to 95% of women – making your hips look wider, creating a muffin-top and keeping you from having a neat, smooth tailored look because most shirts are too blousey and not fitted. Jeans that fit right at the hip are okay. Jeans always look better if they are starched with a crisp crease. It makes you look more professional! She should always be wearing a long sleeved western-type shirt (with the sleeves buttoned), belt, boots, hat and crown. Boots should be polished and her hat should be clean and free of dust. Our girl is asked to wear Wrangler products, as they are a huge sponsor of rodeo and of the queening world, and we believe in riding for the brand.

Makeup should be appropriate for the occasion. We don't want a title holder to look like a hoochie mama, but she should have on makeup products that accentuate her attributes and hide those she may not be so proud of. Always have lipstick on, but not necessarily red, unless it looks good on you!

Hair should be fixed, not hanging straight. The big hair of a few years ago is pretty much gone, but soft curls, or curls at the end, at least show that you made some effort to look pretty. I personally prefer hair pulled back in a ponytail for any time she is in the arena; she is working, not just looking pretty. In short – Nothing is worse than a girl in a beautiful crown who looks sloppy and like she never looked in the mirror before leaving the house.

Manners – At our clinic we even teach the art of proper etiquette, because I expect royalty to know proper manners, whether it be dining etiquette or business etiquette. When wearing that crown, the queen may be seated at the head table during a luncheon or next to the mayor or the Commissioner of the PRCA at an official dinner. If she is not polite and doesn't have proper manners, she just causes a loss of respect for the title, which the next girl will have to deal with. A well placed "yes mam" or appropriate "no sir" will gain a lot of respect and cause a young woman to be remembered in the future.

Puncuality -- I am a stickler for our titleholder to be on time to every appearance or event. Plan to leave earlier if she has to, but NEVER BE LATE! There may be people counting on or waiting for her, so it is imperative that she be punctual. She is told to contact the rodeo in advance to ensure what time she needs to be there and where to be.

Doing her job – When a young woman signs the contract to run for the title of Miss Turquoise Circuit, I make certain that she understands that this is a job she is applying for; a busy and demanding job. For the period of one year, she must follow the rules set forth for MTC, and perform the duties outlined in the contract; none of which are unreasonable. In our case, the title involves being the official spokeswoman for the Turquoise Pro Rodeo Circuit of the Professional Rodeo Cowboys Association. She must travel the states of Arizona and New Mexico talking to the public about our sport and promoting it. She must be able to handle animal rights advocates and know who to refer them to at the rodeo if necessary. MTC has in her job description to contact the arena director and/or stock contractor immediately upon arrival at a rodeo to see where they need her and what they want her to do. While she is at a rodeo, working for the committee and contractor are her job, and her number one priority. They may want her going to schools, talk to people at the mall, or just work the rodeo by carrying flags or shagging cattle. She is there to help them and only that. She should always remember that whatever she does reflects on the next girls to wear the crown. (I know of one major rodeo in Arizona, that because a certain titleholder did not do her job caused them to deny any queen from working their rodeo). It's a big job, but one she applied for and was hired.

Being a queen director can be tough if you don't have a good girl, but one of the most rewarding jobs in the world if you do. I have been so very fortunate to have had the greatest girls in the world to hold the title while I have been the Director of the Miss Turquoise Circuit Pageant. The girls are ambitious, fun, beautiful, and hard-working, and they have made my job so very easy. I wish girls like mine for every director.

From *Dick Reason:*

One important part of these competitions is the personal interview. This is the scariest and most nerve wracking part of the pageant. You have to go into a room and face a bunch of strangers. They are going to ask you questions about almost anything. Your job is to be calm, cool and relaxed.

Some judges will just leave you standing until you ask "May I sit down?" If they have left your chair turned backwards, turn it so it and you face the judges. Always introduce yourself. Ask your queen directors if you should shake hands or not.

You will have a million thoughts going through your head so just take a small quiet breath and try to relax. I discourage contestants from wearing blouses or jackets with fringe on them. It is too easy to play with it and that shows nervousness. We understand that you may be nervous. Answer the questions to the best of your ability, but don't try to over answer. Remember to use good grammar and avoid "verbal garbage", i.e. like, you know and other slang.

If you are asked a question that you don't know the answer to, say so. If you tell the judge who asked the question "I'll look it up and get back to you, DO IT! There are usually some areas where judges can add a couple points into your score for keeping your word.

From *Bob Hays:*

If at all possible, go into the interview room early. Orient yourself, take a good look around. This will help eliminate any visual distractions during the interview itself.

1. Enter the interview with a smile. Relax.
2. Make eye contact with the judges.
3. Sit relaxed, sit properly with good posture.
4. Use correct grammar. Street slang is unacceptable.
5. If you don't know an answer, admit it, but don't be afraid to ask what the answer is.
6. Know your rodeo, local sponsors, history, stock contractor, contract personnel ,and performance schedule
7. At all times be courteous.
8. Be concise, just answer the questions.
9. When you fill out your "biographical" statement, which the judges receive, do not include anything you are not prepared to defend.
10. As an ambassador of rodeo, you should know the rules that govern the sport.
11. Be aware of animal welfare issues.
12. Ask questions if given the opportunity.
13. If asked a questions and you don't understand, don't be afraid to ask for clarification.

14. Be yourself, let your personality shine, you don't get a second chance to make a first impression.

> "I've covered a lot of country in my time, but when you take a man's money you ride for the brand."
>
> *Conagher* **by Louis L'Amour**

Chapter 3

SPONSORS

Some girls obtain sponsors before they run for their first title, to be able to raise funds to buy top quality clothes, pay for speech and riding lessons, and travel expenses. Others wait until after they have won a title, to get sponsors to help with travel costs, more clothes for appearances, and to be able to run for higher titles. TIP: Quality does not always mean expensive.

I'm going to tell you a story about a rodeo queen. She did really well and honestly earned the title. She was being raised by her single father. He had no idea, nor did the rodeo committee tell him, he had to get sponsors. They didn't tell him that the committee didn't have the money to keep her on the road. He lost his job. He didn't know how to go about asking for money. He thought it was like begging. It's an honorable thing to go to a sponsor to present your program and why you are doing this and how you can help the sponsor. He went to the queen director with his daughter. There were a lot of tears. She had to resign. You don't want that. She won honestly, but because of finances, she had to quit. Again, sponsorship can be the life blood of rodeo queens and teen queens. It's something you need to work at all the time. It's something that is so difficult to do. It was so difficult for me and I'm a grown woman with grandchildren. But I had to do it because I believe in the program. No one person is always right. Take these suggestions to heart. Look around your area and see what your area is like economically. See what you can do. See what is expected of you, and if you can truly handle it mentally, physically, emotionally, and financially. Like I said, this is like something you have never experienced before.

To talk to sponsors, you can't just go into a place of business dressed in flip-flops and shorts, and ask, "Would you like to sponsor me as your home town rodeo queen?" You will be guaranteed a big fat NO. Why? Because you did not take the job of getting sponsors seriously, so why should the prospective sponsor take you seriously. See why you need a game plan? I suspect your head is spinning with dollar signs. You now need sponsors and/or to win the lottery. Winning the lottery ...... Chances not so good. Getting sponsors ...... Much better and bigger odds. Take a deep breath and get started.

It is important in sponsorship to have a "game plan." So here are some ideas to help you prepare.

Preparing a presentation book: This idea came from Miss Rodeo Arizona 2007, Katie Hill, and this book alone netted her $15,000.00. In my pocket book that's a whole lot of money. Find a good, thick three ring binder notebook in an attractive color. One with a plastic cover works well so you can slip in a picture of yourself, your town, or your rodeo. You can use a picture of last year's rodeo program cover. Anything which you feel will capture the attention of prospective sponsors.

You've got your book and you've got the tab divider sheets. I would advise to have a table of contents, with a yellow checkmark or yellow square by one topic, and another one with green and another with red, and so on. Put tabs by each one that correlates with a section.

At home get down the keepsakes, the boxes that all families keep of their awards, achievements in 4-H, gymkhana, junior rodeo, church activities, and academic achievements. Do you volunteer at the humane society, cancer society, or do other volunteer work? Have you won awards for raising rabbits at the fair? If the certificates are too large to put into the book, take them to an office supply store. Most of them have machines where they can shrink it down to a reasonable size. If it's for the best lop eared rabbit and you have your blue ribbon, take a photo of it and shrink it down to where the photo of the blue ribbon can be on the bottom horizontally or vertically and put the ribbon photo and the certificate together, so they can see that you try and that you work at something. I also suggest putting these pages in chronological order.

Remember, your prospective sponsors are very busy. They are giving up their time just to listen to you. So make it business like. Keep it simple for them. If you have pictures, put them in, like a little scrapbook He or she can glance down the table of contents and see community service is in green. He can flip green over and see you at the humane society, collecting food for the food bank, fund raising for the cancer society, etc.. It makes the book interesting. They won't feel like they are wasting their time. By doing so, it will also show that you are not afraid to talk to people, work hard, and accomplish something. That will also impress your prospective sponsors.

Keep it tidy. You may want to go to a scrap book store. You don't want a lot of frills, but you do want it very orderly and attractive. You don't want a busy background to detract from the information that is there. You also want to have an interesting ending.

Now practice a meeting. Have someone pretend they are a prospective sponsor/business person. Sit at the kitchen table or dinning room table. Pretend this is the office of the prospective sponsor. You are applying for sponsorship. When asking for an interview, you should be in western attire. That means starched and creased jeans, a crisp western shirt, and a bling belt. You're going in first to make your appointment. Ask one of the clerks if you can speak to the manager or owner. If they say, that he or she are in a meeting, which is often said, if they don't want to be bothered, say," I realize that they are very busy but I would appreciate

15 minutes of time I can show (him or her) where I can promote their business to the general public throughout our state." When speaking to a secretary, give her the same speech. Make sure you get that appointment. Be persistent, be pleasant, be courteous, and when you do get the appointment, be gracious. Verify the time you are to be there.

You can have sibling or friend act as the clerk or secretary. You can have a girlfriend or someone else act as the adult if you are under 18. The secretary or clerk tells the owner or manager "the rodeo queen is here". You walk in, extend your hand and say, "Hello Mrs. Jones, It's so nice to meet you. Thank you for taking time to see me. I'm Suzy Q and I am your local rodeo queen. May I sit down and chat with you for a few minutes?" As you sit down, lay the presentation book on the sponsor's desk.

Here is how to sit down like a lady: Take your left foot, step back. You should feel the seat of the chair on the back of your leg and slowly sit down, cross your ankles, move your feet slightly to the left or right so your knees won't gap open. Place your hands comfortably in your lap.

Tell them why rodeo is so important to your community. Tip: Go to your local Chamber of Commerce and find out how much money the rodeo brought in to the community last year.

Ask them to look at your presentation book so they can see how dedicated you have been in other subjects. This way, they will know that you are willing to put in the time and effort to succeed in your calling as rodeo queen.

Go over and over the practice interview. Ask questions, like "why do you want to be a rodeo queen?" Answer: "Yes, it is fun to make new friends and travel, but I feel strongly that rodeo is THE AMERICAN SPORT and is important to our community's economy."

You have to study your rodeo organization's rulebook, know the history of rodeo, why we have the events, livestock welfare, how well the animals are treated. Rodeo is a part of American history. Talk to the sponsor and let them know what you can do for them.

Tell them "There will be radio, newspaper and television interviews. I will have my signature sheets, which will list all the sponsors on the back.

When practicing the sponsor interviews, make sure your grammar is good. As my husband says, "no garbage", no ummms, or uhhhs, or ya knows, before each sentence. Watch for twiddling your thumbs, squirming in the chair, playing with any fringe on your shirt, or twirling your hair. No playing with cuffs on the shirt. Don't forget to video record every single practice. Simply watch for anything that would distract the sponsor from what you are asking for and why you are asking for it.

Listen to see if your voice is squeaky, too loud, or too soft. Pay close attention to your enunciation and pronunciation. Good grammar always impresses sponsors. You need to speak clearly and in a positive manor.

You need to have confidence and speak with an even voice, no giggling because people sometimes giggle when they are nervous, and, *Absolutely no gum.*

This has to be done over and over so it is so automatic for you that when you go to your first sponsor, you will not be nervous. Practice with others. Video record every session and review it. You might be playing with the papers in your notebook before you hand it to the prospective sponsor. You will also hear if your voice was shaky. You might think that wasn't so bad, but then when you see yourself in the video, you will think, "oh my goodness, it wasn't nearly as good as I thought it was." Do it again and again until it's perfect. When you feel it is perfect, you should take the video to your school and show it to the drama coach, English teacher or the speech teacher. Ask if they would watch this short video and critique it.

You need to be the most polished professional, impressive young woman that they have seen. You need to stick in their mind for good reasons, not because you can pop gum really loud. Think about it. It takes a lot of time to be really good.

Then let someone else be the prospective sponsor and they are going to act really bored, play with a pencil as you go on. Hand them the book and they may not seem interested, you just keep chatting most pleasantly. Remember you are the one who is applying. Not the rodeo queen director, not the rodeo committee members, you are the independent business woman and are asking for sponsorship and telling the sponsor what you can give them in return. Try to think of every possible scenario you can run into. There might be a lot of resistance. Anything they can give you, product or monetary, is most greatly appreciated.

When you leave, extend your hand, shake their hand and thank them for their time, and for the visit, and hand them the pamphlet on Livestock welfare. Then say goodbye, and leave the office.

To find prospective sponsors, first look in the phone book. Count how many businesses are in the yellow pages. Say if you have 300 businesses, and they each donate a dollar, that's $300 and that's better than zero. Think outside of the box; always think outside of the box. Try new things.

Here are some tips on how to dress for your meeting. I live in the southwest and we wear broomstick skirts and Spanish influenced blouses, neckerchiefs, bead work from the Indians, etc. Let's say you're from Nebraska. I don't know if prairie skirts are still popular back there. Maybe you're just as comfortable in a pair of starched jeans. If plaid is popular in your area, or a very simple long sleeved, colored shirt, wear it. You are talking to sponsors of your area. Don't wear a blouse with saguaros on it. Saguaros grow naturally in the northern part of the Sonoran desert and that's where Arizona is. It would look pretty silly if someone from Arizona wore a shirt of sunflowers, like Kansas or wheat fields from Nebraska. If it's not typical of your area, don't wear it! You are representing your area. You are inviting people to come to your home town rodeo, to your state, to spend some time, enjoy the people and shop at your sponsors' place of business. If you live in an area where there is a lot of humidity, which we don't have here in my state, you don't have to wear the fluffy queen hair. Pull it back at the nape of the neck, make sure it's clean and secure it with a nice, attractive clip.

You should wear your banner and crown, if you are a title holder, and just a nice plaid or plain colored western shirt or, if your area wears button down collars, and wear a good pair of starched jeans with a nice crease. When you go out on business, always wear appropriate western style clothes. Now, whether you are running for the title or if you have the title, people are going to be highly critical, especially your sponsors, because word, good or bad, is going to get back to them. I'm afraid that shorts and flip flops and tank tops are in the background. Wear them at home but you can't wear them in public. People are going to make comments that they would never have made if you were just an ordinary teenager going to the park with friends or going to the movies or whatever activity you may do. You have to be on your guard at all times because people are going to be judging you. If you take your mom with you, have her dress western too. They put the two of you together. You don't have to be twins but you do have to be aware of what people are going to say. Now, this is my opinion, some people may have a different opinion.

Don't take your mother into sponsor presentation. If you are young enough to need her she can drive you and make sure the book is clean and tidy and things are in order with all of your awards and achievements and that it states what your future goals are.

Whether you are alone, or have your queen director or a member of the rodeo committee, you are the main speaker. You have to show them that you are capable of handling all the responsibilities that are required of the queen or teen queen. You are now an independent business woman and that's how it has to be seen. If the sponsor agrees to give you, say a hundred dollar check, you are responsible to show them how you will be spending their money.

Make sure there is no makeup on the inside of your collar. Make sure the crease on your pants is straight, that your skirt isn't too long, your boots are polished, and your hands are clean with nails nicely polished. This is a face to face interview. If you have naturally rosy cheeks, don't put more blush on them. Put a tiny bit of eye shadow on to make your eyes sparkle and a tiny bit of colored lip gloss, for shine and sparkle. It shows maturity. I keep coming back to that. You're going to find a lot of that in this book but that's how you learn and how you remember. It's that important that it has to be restated over and over again.

If you are going to wear cologne, two squirts from the bottle are sufficient. Three or four are too much because we don't want them to smell you before you arrive. You just want it to be subtle. Make sure your boots are clean. I know I have said that already, but you would be amazed at how many judges check that. If you're wearing jeans, make sure the cuffs are not frayed. If that's all you have, borrow a pair from friends. There is nothing wrong with borrowing clothes. The ladies from Miss Rodeo America borrow and buy from each other all the time. You can do the same thing. Make sure it fits well. You don't want hip huggers that go way below the belly or the high waist that gives you a high pocket look. An in between look is just fine. A bling belt is perfectly fine to make you look a bit sparkling. Wear some nice earrings and make sure your hat has been dusted and well-shaped. Make sure your shirt is clean at the cuffs. Tuck in your shirt so your appearance is smooth and well groomed. Again, be sure your nails are well groomed and hands are dry. The first impression is the most important one.

Always show up at least 10 minutes before your appointment. When you show up, tell the secretary or clerk, "I realize I am early but I'll just sit here for a few minutes because I know they are busy." Nothing will make your prospective sponsor angrier than if they finally consent to giving you 15 minutes of their busy time and you show up late, forget about everything else, just say," hi I'm Suzy Q" and just go home because basically that's all you're going to get. If you're late, you lost them, so always do your best to be there 10 minutes early with your book.

At the interview, the manager will take you to the office, or if it is a restaurant you might sit at a table. That's what I did. I sat at a table and I got a national sponsor for Miss Rodeo Arizona. I presented my book. I also had the program for the previous year. I talked to them about the quality of young women who were running. Let them look at the book. I talked about the duties she has, all the traveling she will be doing and how their company's name will be mentioned over and over again. By now you should be instructed well enough on how to conduct yourself in a businesslike manner. In the preparation you have gone over and over this. You have videoed it and had it critiqued by people who are educated in this field.

When you go to the interview, you need to let the sponsors know what you will be doing, where you will be traveling, and whom you will be talking to. You need to let them know that there may be television interviews, radio interviews, talking to the newspaper. Let the sponsor know that their name will be given out in public all the time, especially when you pass out your autograph sheet, which is your picture sheet. Let them know if you will have a sign that will be on the side of your horse trailer or truck, that will say "Miss Roundup Days Rodeo Queen from Rattlesnake Gulch, visit our town and our sponsors". Then, on the truck or trailer, have all of your sponsors listed. They work hard for their money so you have to show them that you will give them free advertisement in return.

You need to watch your grammar. Have your book ready and if you are nervous about it, before you go in, a little trick is to keep some baby wipes in your vehicle and wipe your hands so they will be all nice and dry so that when you shake hands, you will appear to be a mature, calm, and well prepared young woman. A cold hand is always an indication that you are very scared and they may take pity on you but they may also not take you seriously.

I know I keep emphasizing clean hands, clean and well-shaped hat, new looking cuffs on your jeans, clean collars, and shirt cuffs, a well pressed professional appearance etc., I just can't emphasize enough just how important a first impression is! No matter what else may follow, that first impression will always stick in their minds. Everything else will be vague memories.

You can start the conversation with, "I ran for rodeo queen, not just because it would be fun and I will make new friends, but because I feel strongly about educating the public about rodeo and, to preserve rodeo. I will be letting people know about the PRCA's 63 laws to protect the rodeo livestock."

Try your best to make this interview brief. I know there's a lot going on here, but you don't want to take 20 or 30 minutes of their time. They're busy and that will irritate them slightly and you will be less likely to get their sponsorship.

After they have looked at the book and they say, "all right, I'll give you a $100.00 check", you thank them graciously, stand up, extend your hand again and say "Thank you Mrs. Jones. It has been a pleasure."

It's very important that you do a good job with your presentation because if you do a poor job, it will be more difficult for the girl that follows you to acquire sponsorship.

You will want to keep in your binder notebook, a list of everyone who has sponsored you. The more names you have the more impressive it will be to another prospective sponsor.

To thank your sponsors, you might want to have a barbeque. It might be before the rodeo at the rodeo grounds, or even in your back yard. It doesn't matter if they gave you products, $5.00 or $500.00. No one needs to know how much they donated. Call the paper, call the TV station, call the radio station. Let them know that you are having a thank you dinner for your sponsors. You can invite them to share the food. If they don't show up, you can take the pictures. You write the story about how everyone came and what a great time it was. You can offer your thanks publicly for those who supported you.

If you don't have a dinner, to show your appreciation for their sponsorship, send thank you notes or certificates of appreciation. Have your photograph shrunk down to where it is small, whatever suits the certificate. You can buy them at the office supply store. Put it in a nice inexpensive frame and present it to them.

If you are going to present it to them in person, call the TV, radio stations, or newspapers to see if they can be there. If they say they don't have time, I'll tell you what I did; I just bugged the sports director at our local TV station. I said our queen is going to be in your local rodeo parade. Could you just take two minutes to interview her? You're going to be down on the road there interviewing the audience about how they love the parade and their favorite part. They could interview her during the parade. She could lean over and say, "I'm having the time of my life; this is a fun rodeo parade, I'm so glad to be here".

The newspaper said, no, no, no. So what did I do? I sent the article anyway with a teacup containing roses and the photograph of our queen and I got 2 inches in the paper. It might not sound like much but I got something in the paper. So, don't give up. Don't ever give up.

If you didn't win, just send a thank you note.

All right, here you go girl. You are going to hit the rodeo trail. You're going to spend the money and use the products that your sponsors gave you. It is very important, and I stress very important, that you go back periodically, if they're busy leave a note for them. Don't take up their time but always have pictures of what you used their money for. As I said before, you are an independent business woman. Keep the books. Know who paid you, how much they paid you and have a page in your accounting book for each sponsor and what their product or money did to help you be more successful. That way you are honest, open about it and they will be pleased to know that they have helped you. It will also make it easier for the new girl that follows. Keep a list of those sponsors. Don't expect that poor girl to go through what you had to go through. I can give you an example of that.

There was a state queen and boy did she work hard and she placed in the top five at the national competition, so she was quite good. This young lady kept a record of who were her sponsors, what they gave her and how she spent it. She made three copies of this record of her finances. She gave them to her state board and naively she didn't keep a copy for herself. Guess what the board members did with them? One lost it and two threw them in the trash. When the new queen was elected and she was signing her contract, they said "now honey, you are going to have to go and find your own sponsors". You never know what people are going to do. It's sad, but regrettably it's the truth. This young lady was hurt. She put forth a lot of effort, she stuck her neck out.

This young lady asked every one of her sponsors if they would be willing to sponsor the new state queen and 80% of them said yes. So, if you do this, my suggestion would be give a copy of the record to the new queen. Remember, moral standards, quality, intelligent, clean, charming young lady, who doesn't gossip, is what sponsors are looking for.

> **"A good horse is never a bad color"**
>
> ***Savvy saying*** **By Ken Alstad**

CHAPTER 4

HORSEMANSHIP COMPETITION

*Part **A**:*

Horsemanship is much more than just learning how to ride a horse. This is a living, breathing animal. When my husband started judging, friends and their young daughters would come to us and say, "Would you help us buy a horse? This looks like so much fun." His answer would always be the same. "Tell you what, do you have a relative or a neighbor or a friend who has a child that is about 2 or 3 years old. Go to them and say I want to be the nanny for a whole week. I will play with your child, I will feed them, I will change the diapers, I will bathe them, I will get up with them in the middle of the night, and I will read stories to them, everything a parent does. I would like to care for them for a week and give you a break." So she gets the job as the nanny for one whole week. Then he would say to them, "When you are finished, this is my phone number call me and we will go look for a horse". Not surprisingly, no one has ever called.

It's a huge responsibility to take care of a domestic animal. These are not wild animals on the range. These are domesticated horses. They've been broke. That's kind of an odd saying, being broke. This means they have been conditioned or trained. I like the word trained to ride, to have you on their back. They look forward to seeing you come at feeding time. Clean their water tanks, brush them, check their hoofs every day. Know a good farrier. Go to your veterinarian and make sure they get at least their annual vaccinations and Coggins blood test. If you are on a state line, and take your horse across the state line, you can't cross that line without the Coggins blood test. There are a lot of things to consider. There is a tremendous amount of information from the veterinarian. You don't need to know all of it. That's why I said this is the yellow relipsionary book. It's going to last you a long time and as you go from contest to contest and circuit and state and someday, if you are interested, competing for Miss Rodeo America or Miss Rodeo U.S.A. You are going to go back to this information over and over again. Some of it will never be old. There are certain things that are just plain, basic common sense information, so, do read it. Another personal note, before we get going on the bulk of this chapter, see if you are fortunate enough to have a stock contractor, like the Honeycutt Rodeo Inc. they always have a horse for a queen who is unable to bring their own. Listen to your stock contractor about the horse. Find out what kind of a bitt is use, what kind of a mouth the horse has, if they love to run hard, and if they are a pickup horse. The advice from this stock contractor was don't exercise and warm them up for an hour. They said five or ten minutes max because they are working horses. They are already warmed up. This is just to get them used to you and you used to the horse.

Most rodeos start with bareback riding, and these pick up horses are going to have to run after that bucking horse and pick up the cowboy, and they won't want to do it if they have already been worked. Check with your stock contractor because they don't always start with the same events.

Consider the horse at all times, his health, his energy and every single day go out and check them. Lay your hands on them and make sure there aren't any scratches or burs on them. Make sure they are exercised every day. How would you like to be stuck in your bedroom all day every day? It wouldn't be much fun, would it? Think of it that way. Work your horse every day. Go to your vet and let them know what you're going to be doing. Find out what to feed them. The feed is going to change according to the activity of the horse. I've also taken this chapter and divided it into sections. My guest writers will be addressing these sections. One is on how to ride as rodeo royalty and that takes some practice. The next one is learn how to read a horse. It might sound kind of silly but you need to know what the best qualities of that horse are and utilize it when you do your free style pattern in the competition. Some competitions let you use your horse and some competitions furnish horses for first, the reigning pattern then a different horse for a free style patters or rail work. Most often this is done in circuit or state competitions.

If you don't know what a reigning pattern is, you can look it up on line and look up the American Quarter Horse Association. They have all the reigning patterns there. You never know which one you are going to get. Be familiar with them and let the horse be familiar with them.

Walk the arena. You don't have to take your horse in it. See where there are dips and rocks. If it's a windy day, if the sponsor flags along the sides are flapping you might want to take your horse in because it can be quite unnerving for them. Walk them around and let them get used to it. A judge suggested, stay about three (3) feet from the railing. You don't want to get so close that you hurt your ankle or your knee. Learn what a hot lap is. That's when you are announced and you go in full gallop and waive to the audience. This is where your training comes in on learning how to ride as rodeo royalty. You don't want to fall off your horse. You should be seated solidly, running fast and waiving to the audience. You should ask the queen director if you ride in and ride right out of the arena or if you ride in and stay in the middle of the arena until all queens are in the middle. After the announcer says," let's give all of these ladies a hand," the last one in will lead out or sometimes the first one in will lead out. Ask the queen director. Always double check how she wants it or ask the person in charge of the grand entry because they might also be handling the hot laps.

Flag runs; know what a flag boot is. It is a boot that attaches to the stirrup leather. The flag boot is made to hold a pole that holds a flag. Don't push the flag forward and don't let it lean back. Try very hard, and it is hard, to keep it straight. You don't want your arm way up high by the flag. Try to keep your hand slightly higher than your shoulder so you have control. Again, here is something else that needs to be practiced and practiced. Some horses don't like that flag flapping around their head. Let them sniff it, let them get used to it, go slow and work your way up to a full gallop. Remember, it was like taking care of that 3 year old, it just takes time for them to get used to the flag. Let them learn not to be afraid.

Chapter10 will cover knowledge of equine illnesses, the signs of illnesses and the treatments. There will be a picture of the anatomy of the horse. Don't forget to call the PRCA to get the livestock information that will explain a little bit about their nervous systems and how different their skin is compared to human skin. All of this is important because you are going to encounter members of PETA and SHARK. These people are militant and are against rodeo. They don't understand how well the stock contractors take care of their stock. You need to be well prepared to counter whatever any of these groups have to say, so study, study, study. I've said that before, but that's why I've always said that it's good to have a year before you run. If you have just a few months, then go for it. The experience itself will be invaluable and it will help so much for your run the following year if you don't win your first year. You will have fewer nerves and so will your horse.

Now we come to dress for the horsemanship competition. Check the package your queen director is going to send you. Some of the pageant directors prefer white western shirts and dark wrangler jeans. If you're wearing black boots or brown boots, you may have white stitching from the sole of the boot, just get some permanent markers and color the threads. It won't hurt the boots and it will last even on a rainy day. It won't run and it won't be disturbing to the eyes of the judges. You'll have a nice clean line.

Also, some competitions like to see you in colored outfits. According to Miss Rodeo America Inc. they prefer a chromatic color scheme. Say that peach is a gorgeous color on you; peach shirt, peach pants and yes, you are going to have to dye those boots peach. If you are wearing a white hat, the boots can be white to match the hat. The clothing should be monochromatic. Avoid stripes and plaids because they will show the slightest mistake and that will catch the judge's eye. Solid colors are best but you can have a little sparkle on the shoulders, the sleeves or on the front but don't have it clear down the back. In the southwest sometimes we have a stripe down the side of the leg, very formal, very attractive, but boy is it going to show every little mistake that you might make. Get your packet and read it so that you won't be embarrassed by not knowing what to expect. You need to be comfortable and know exactly what you are supposed to do. Times are changing. Nothing is stagnant in rodeo, even though it goes back so long ago. Queens used to have extremely curly, fluffy hair but styles have changed. Contact your rodeo association and see what they are asking the girls to do. Straight hair, long hair, short hair, fluffy hair; know what is expected and what is appropriate at the time you compete.

Most importantly, know how to keep your hat on. I use duct tape. I take a strip and place the sticky side on the sweat band in the front of the hat. This strip never comes off. Now I take a longer strip of duct tape, roll it in a circle so it will stick to itself, sticky out. Place this piece of duct tape to the piece of duct tape that is already stuck to the hat. Make sure your hair around your forehead is moved off your forehead. Make sure the tape is stuck tight to your forehead. Take bobby pins and pin the hat onto your hair from ear to ear. Make sure the hat has a bite to it. A bite means that it is just slightly smaller than you want. When you put it on your head it feels like there is a rubber band around it and when you put the duct tape and bobby pins on, it <u>will</u> stay.

It was so embarrassing at one grand entry the queen director told the girls how to put their hats on so they won't lose them in the arena. She gave them a "welcome kit" that had duct tape in it and bobby pins. What did these girls do at that competition? They said that's going to hurt with that duct tape so all they used were the bobby pins. When they were introduced and they did their hot lap, there went the hat. Flopping on the back of their head with 2 or 3 bobby pins and the crown went flying in the dirt. Most hats will fall off even with a few bobby pins left on. Embarrassing? Mercy yes! Know how to keep that hat on. Don't ever lose your hat or your crown in the arena.

There is so much to learn, but these are the little things that will keep you looking proper, polished and well groomed. This way people will be anxious to talk to you instead of saying, "I bet you were embarrassed when you lost your hat and crown." No, you don't want that. Know what to do at all times.

Makeup: Now this is a little different than when you went in for sponsorship interviews and it will be different than when you model and give your speeches. You are in the arena and the audience is far away. Use a brighter shade of the color you used for the sponsor interview. Outline the eyes so that they can be seen but not always in a dark black. Gear the makeup to your age. Make absolutely sure you have sunscreen on. One young lady did not wear sunscreen during horsemanship and she sun burned. Her modeling dress was pink and purple. She just blended into that dress. You couldn't tell where the girl stopped and the dress began. Always get a good sunscreen, not a low SPF, use a 30 or 50. It sounds ridiculous but it works. You can also buy creams that are tinted that have sun screen in them, use both. You can also get lipstick that has sunscreen. When you first put the sunscreen on, don't forget your lips and ears. You have to take care of yourself. Take care of your hair and take care or your skin.

Okay, are you beginning to get the picture? Since I am such an expert on falling off a horse, I thought I would have experts on how to stay on a horse. This is very important if you are going to be a rodeo queen. It would be kind of silly if you ran around with a stick horse. Pay attention to what they have to say. It will make your reign most enjoyable and so much easier.

Always have your kit packed and check it before you leave home, just as you would for your horse.

Make sure you have everything you need for your horse. If you want to put ribbons in the horse's mane, make sure they are packed. If he just got over an infection, make sure you have some extra medication in case it returns. Make sure he has all his vaccinations. It's not possible to keep your horse away from other horses, especially in the grand entry. Go to your equine veterinarian and have your horse taken care of properly.

The veterinarian's material is going to be a little heavy sometimes. There is a section on vaccinations, how much water, how much feed, how much grain, read all of that part. Some of it is going to be a little more detailed and more for if you are running for circuit or when you decide to run for state, then Miss Rodeo America or Miss Rodeo USA. You don't have to read all of it, just know where it is. Remember, you don't have to know everything, just know where to find the answers.

Here are some Savvy Sayings by Ken Alstad and I think they are rather cute:

"When in doubt let your horse do the thinking". I think sometimes that is very true. The horse is smarter than some of the girls, but I'm sure you are quite bright.

"You've got to control yourself before you can control your horse".

Think about it. If you can't control your temper, if you can't control your nerves, that's going to transmit to that horse and you're going to have a bad time at the rodeo, so you have to control yourself before you can control your horse. Don't say "I should have done this or I should have done that". If the horse isn't willing to do it right now, he isn't going to do it. You go back to the trainer who is experienced, who has had winners, and ask him, "how do I correct this problem?"

Keep one eye on the judge and one eye on those who work in the arena."

Anonymous

Arena Eteiquett:

Part B:

The following people are knowledgeable in their field of expertize. Jim Fain is a well know Rodeo Photographer and Black and white western art photographer. He is in the Utah Hall of Fame.

From Jim Fain:

Hazards

As a rodeo photographer I face many Hazards in the arena. Quoting rodeo photographer Louise Serpa, "Don't never not pay attention." You will get run over by not heeding that advice.

One of the those hazards is not as obvious as a kick bucking horse or a hard charging bull… it's the rodeo queen "HOT LAP". Queens make their introduction runs around the arena in a full out gallop, in a semi trance. They have a frozen smile, a mechanical wave and a blurred vision of thousands of faces surrounding the open space of the arena. They have little awareness of other human beings along the side lines.

While there is a certain risk involved photographing queen runs, it comes with the territory. You have to be a little more exposed to their run to get a great head-on photo. I've had them blow by with inches, nothing close.

They have to touch you for it to be close.

Judges are another story. They are more vulnerable being deep in thought about the last score, while concentrating|on getting quickly to the timed event end of the arena. I personally know one judge who got drilled by a queen and suffered a badly broken femur.

My closest really bad scare occurred not while photographing queen runs, but while acting as a judge. I'm hoofin' it for the timed event end and get stopped by the last bareback rider out, asking about his score. At the same time, Miss Rodeo America is launching her intro run from the timed event end. She reads the situation and plans her run to pass between me and the fence. I look up in time to see nothing but a three foot spread of buck skin horse chest, in a dead run...my instant reaction...go for the fence! I felt the wind ripple my shirt, but she never touched me.

Tip: Now according to one rodeo queen judge, Dick Reason, stay about three (3) feet from the fence, always look ahead and to avoid the above situation go around the judge and contestant and not between the fence and the judge.

I spoke to **Mr. Bronc Rumford.** He is a Past president of Miss. Rodeo America, and the owner of Runford Rodeo Co.

When I asked him, " What is the first thing you would say to a Group of contestants?" Without hesitation, he said, " Be Prepared!" What a mouthful! Study all there is to know, know what it means, and when to do it.

Here is some of the things we talked about: In horsemanship find a good teacher for the QUEEN SEAT. This is very different then pleasure riding. An easy way is to go to the coach who helped a young lady win hoesemanship.

Know the American Quarter Horse Association standardfor horsemanship competition. This will be useful for the set pattern and your free style pattern. Tip: you may have a different horse for free style and plan "A." may not work for the second horse, so have a plan "B."

When you are given your packet check the set pattern that will be used. You and your horse will need to practice this over and over again. Remember " BE PREPARED."

My next writer is Miss. Rodeo U.S.A. 2000 for the International Professional Rodeo Association,

Marjon Brady Brown

HORSEMANSHIP

A rodeo queen would simply be a queen without a horse. That is why the horsemanship category is highly sought after. Many rodeo queens earn a badge of honor by being a great horse-woman. Rightfully so, since they are representing our western lifestyle and traditions.

Hopefully, you feel right at home in the saddle, and if you do, this part of the competition will very natural to you. If you struggle with your horsemanship, this part of the pageant could make you a little less than confident. However, with practice leading to perfection, mixed with hours spent in the saddle, you can be confident in your abilities.

I am a big advocate for a unique identity that will separate you from the rest of the contestants. I was honored to wear my grandmother's clothes that she wore as she Reno Rodeo Queen 50 years earlier when I competed for Miss Rodeo U.S.A. That definitely made memorable impression to the judges and I felt so much confidence wearing her clothes. Do and be refreshingly different while still being very professional, in style and true to who you are. Do what you can to project one of a kind personality, to the audience all the way the best seat in the house – from the back of that horse.

Tips For Before The Competition:

Do ride along and learn from farriers, Vets., horse chiropractors etc. Spending a handful of hours with them can be more valuable then reading it in a book or trying to learn it on your own. Where possible , take classes on equine science from a community college or university.

Study up on all horse related topics: equine science, diseases, care, Nutrition, rodeo terminology, rodeo history, rodeo rulebooks, equine conformation & anatomy, animal welfare facts, and a knowledge of tack & different types of bits, just to name a few.

Ride as many " borrowed " horses as you can. However, make certain you do not try to ride beyond your abilities, or push past the horse's ability. That can be an invitation for a horse accident.

Learning to "read" a horse can take a lifetime. Nearly each twitch of the ear is communicating something valuable if we can learn to pick on up it. Pay attention to all the horse's signals.

Study and dissect each pattern in depth beforehand. Follow each precise detail. If it says to settle your horse for a certain amount of time, then do just that. Perform the pattern as it is written, unless otherwise directed.

*A word of caution-if you will be competing on your own horse do not over-practice the pattern to the point that your horse anticipates every move.

If you know who your judges are going to be before the pag- eant, learn what you can about their bios. If they are a horse show judge, they are likely to pay attention to detail to your pattern and seat. If they are a farrier,it is likely at least one horsemanship question will be about the hoof.

Practice your mount and dismount several times during each Preparation ride on different horse heights. If you are confident with a jump mount and can do it smooth and consistent each time, then do it. For those woman who think they "are not strong enough to do a jump mount," it is not about Strength. Do not get discouraged. It is far more about your form and leverage. Anyone can jump mount with the right instruction.

Ride one handed as often as possible leading up to the pageant so it is natural to you.

Video tape yourself doing the patterns, hot laps and waving. Review it to critique it.

Graciously accept any suggestions and help from horse trainers and professionals. Perhaps not all their suggestions will apply to rodeo queen completion, but the more you learn, the more versatile of a rider you will become. You will be surprised what clues and tricks you can learn and apply on different types of horses.

Taci Shaffer , Miss Rodeo Arizona 2014, and the horsemanship winner for Miss Rodeo America, said she rode one time with 3 different trainers. She took notes at the end of each session which comprised of about 3 things she wanted to make sure to remember and practice. When she went home, she rode at least 1-3 different horses a day, at least 5 days a week. She practiced each pattern and mentally practice each thing from each trainer. She said, "They are such simple reminders , but I feel they really helped. When you are under pressure, it's hard to remember what you learned and naturally just want to react. This really kept my mind right."

If you will be riding your own horse, make certain you do what you can to have your horse and tack look clean and pristine as possible. Use leather cleaning product and toothbrush to get deep into the leather tooling of your tack. If possible match your horses saddle blanket to your wardrobe. Make sure bell boots are clean as well.

Wardrobe:

Strongly examine what color scheme compliments your riding Strengths and even your arena surroundings. If your legs have a lot of movement, be cautious about wearing a neon or white color that would accentuate the movement.

Always pay attention to the rules for horsemanship wardrobe. If it requests you to wear a specific color or have a sponsor on the arm, make sure you do it. Also wearing sponsors clothing is a good idea too, where possible.

Be Monochromatic in Your Color Scheme. Don't wear a belt of a contrasting color that will "cut you in half." Match the belt to your jeans.

Consider dying your belt and boots if necessary. If boots are worn , freshen them up with deep cleaning and make sure you don't leave the heel out of the cleaning.

Make certain you ride in your clothes before the competition Make sure your jeans are not too snug to mount your horse, or that the bottoms of your brand new boots will not slip out of the stirrup. Make sure your arm length is not too short or too long, and that your jeans are long enough to stack, so that they do not ride up your leg when you ride. If you are concerned about that, you can request a seamstress to sew an elastic strip on the bottom of your jeans, that no one can see, so that your paint leg will not rise up.

You can apply slightly heavier makeup and vibrant lipstick for the arena. Arena lights tend to wash people out. Make sure your hat is in keeping with the current rodeo queen trends. Pulling your hair back for horsemanship reduces a bouncy riding appearance.

During the Competition:

Just prior to entering the arena-make sure your hat will not come off under any circumstance. Duck tape and bobby pins will be your best friend. If you still worry about it coming off, fold napkins in the hat liner to make less room for movement. Give your boots one final quick cleaning with a rag before entering the arena. Your feet will most likely be at about eye level to your judges. Make sure your jeans are nicely stacked. A silent personal prayer for safety to do your best can help take the edge off too.

Before beginning the pattern, get the go ahead from the announcer and the judges that they are ready for you to enter the arena.

Consider smiling at the judges and do a slight head nod to demonstrate you are about to beging the pattern. Make eye contact with your judges and audience as you feel comforttable.

During your ride, SMILE AND BREATHE AND CONVEY CONFIDENCE. So many of us are so out of breath when we finally complete the pattern that it takes a minute before we can any questions in the arena.

Use the proper riding position: There should be a straight line from the back of your ear to the back of your heel. Remember, toes up and heels down. Be calm in your riding demeanor, and not stiff. Watch your free hand placement (usually will be in front of your buckle). Do not let your elbows wing out and flap.

The horse is not being judge, but your ability to control the horse and execute the pattern are.

Watch your arena markers, if they are provided. If not, mentally make your own. You can use light poles or fence posts. If the pattern says to hit center, do just that.

Make certain there is a distinguishable speed change if it calls for a small, slow circle and then a fast , large one. Know your pattern speed and size variations. (paying close attention to arena to arena markers and speed changes can be an easy way to impress your judges). If you have a free style pattern, watch the time limits. Do not go beyond. Utilize strengths of both horse and rider for the best pattern. If you have a reiner, capitalize on that with spins/rollbacks/ etc. If you have a horse that does not do flying lead changes, do not have several in the pattern. Make certain you include all elements they call for in the freestyle pattern. Try to have at least one maneuver that is different from the other patterns they will see that day. For example, a diagonal from one end of the arena to the other.

Keep your circles as circles. Make sure they are round and clean. For people who are visual learners, this may help you: Imagine a baseball diamond with 4 bases.

Make certain to LOOK in the direction of the next base and round the line to make a nice clean circle, making certain to hit each base.

Use leg cues when possible, instead of or in addition to, your hands, if the horse responds to it. Lift your hand slightly to que for stops and spins.

Allow the horse to breath between maneuvers and to keep it calm. Don't feel the need to rush through the elements. Try to keep the horse collected.

If the current queen sets the pattern and it differs from the written pattern, find out which way they want it executed.

Make sure your reins are even during the pattern. Work on the best stops for your horse's ability. If you get a sliding stop out of your horse, don't aggressively pursue one Take a deeper seat for a stop so you don't pop out of the saddle. Get your horse to come to a nice clean full stop.

Be cautious, not too aggressive on your horse. The intense competition tends to make rodeo queens have a stronger hand than necessary at times. However, demonstrate that you are in control. If possible, make small corrections as opposed to riding heavy handed as necessary at the very beginning so you do not fluster or confuse your horse from the get go.

Only ride 2 handed when necessary for safety and increased control.

If your horse does not pick up its correct lead immediately, break the horse down and attempt one or 2 more times to showcase that you understand the horse is in the wrong lead. However, using an entire circle to get the correct lead is excessive.

Do your best to set up you horse for flying lead changes. That will be far better than a simple lead change. There are several ways you can "force a horse" into a flying lead change with correct commands. Exaggerate lead changes and move your shoulders with the direction change.

If you are provided a horse, listen to anything and everything the owner's say about it. Ask questions about it if permissible. Watch it intently as it is warmed up. Make mental notes on that horse's strength so you can capitalize on those abilities in the arena.

Signal the completion of your pattern by looking at the judges with a smile.

Approaching the Judges:

Smile as you approach. If for some reason you don't have a Great pattern, do not have a bad attitude. Keep smiling. A judge will remember a negative attitude before they recall a flawed horsemanship pattern.

Once you have dismounted, and you have quietly gathered your reins, and your horse standing as square as possible, get in a flattering stance and answer questions confidently.

Watch your reins. Do not fling them around your horse's neck or let them touch the ground once you are on the ground. Do not loop them around your hand.

Know your horse as best you can. The judges may ask a simple question about your horse's conformation. If it is borrowed, you may not know it unless you studied it beforehand. Be familiar with the tack(for example, what bit you have and why you chose it) and if the tack is well fitted.

Be prepared for the common question "what would you Improve on your pattern, and what did you do well?" It is surprising when girls don't have an answer to that one. That should be a slam dunk. Humility is ideal, but so is being confident. Find the right balance.

Do NOT get flustered if you do not know an answer. Perhaps the judges are asking a question they don't expect you to know the answer to, just watch how you handle it.

ALWAYS do a tack check before mounting.

When you mount and dismount, do not touch the back of the saddle.

Flag Run or Queen's run/ Buzz Run/ Hot lap

Smile. Utilize your presentation and control to the best of your abilities. Use a speed you are comfortable with and a speed safe for the arena. Analyze the ground and how deep/muddy the corners are. Adjust accordingly.

Use the whole arena. Keep your hand at a natural height, it does not need to be far above your head. Do not have a stiff hand and do not wave it carelessly. Try to use a feminine wave that rates well with the cadence of your horse's stride.

Make eye contact with your judges and audience.

Don't lean too far forward, as posture is important.

A head nod or possibly turning your horse around to wave at your audience at the completion of your hot lap portion before leaving the arena shows an awareness to your judges.

Make sure your horse is flag broke before taking a flag. A flag boot (if allowed) is a great tool for a rodeo queen. You can stick it deep into your boot but that requires a lot of control of your mount and a steady seat and hand. Keep the flag upright and don't let it lean backwards. If the flag is large or you are riding with speed, you may need to push it slightly forward so it doesn't throw you back.

Remember-you may be being judged even if it is not an official judging session. Be mindful of you attitude and kindness, and express gratitude to all who helped you during the horsemanship portion.

ALWAYS SMILE, NO MATTER WHAT. Even if a golden rodeo queen rule is broken, such as losing your hat, keep calm and keep smiling, it will go a long way.

I wish you the very best in your endeavors. You are, representing more than just a title whether you win or lose. You are representing our treasured way of life. Do it with grace and kindness, and in so doing, you will already be a winner.

insert image 2

Diagram of a saddle

Ignorance is expensive

Anonymous

CHAPTER 5

PRIVATE INTERVIEW

The interview you had at horsemanship is strictly for horsemanship. Those questions will be asked in the arena or after horsemanship.

Interviews are where you can win or lose a competition. This is where a lot of study must be done in advance. The personal interview portion is the portion of the pageant that enables the judges to evaluate a contestant in a one on one situation. The interview allows the judges to get to see the contestants' personalities and their ability to converse on different subjects. They will judge the contestants on how they feel they will handle these difficult situations with rodeo fans, sponsors, and others they may come in contact with should they win the title. The judges will look for the contestant who is sincere, confident, intelligent and prepared. Just a reminder, this is **not** a beauty contest. It is one of **knowledge.**

When preparing for an interview, a contestant must put herself in the judge's shoes and ask herself, if I were judging, what would I look for? One of the most important things a contestant can do is properly prepare herself in order to go into an interview with confidence. This confidence will come from knowing that you have done your best and utilized all tools available to you to prepare. Even with the best preparation, contestants won't always have all of the answers, but if a contestant has the knowledge that she has done her best to prepare, she will be able to handle not knowing everything with comfort and put the judges at ease with what she does know. With preparation and the confidence that comes with it, the interview can be a tool for a contestant to use to let the judges know that she is the contestant who is prepared and is ready to promote the sport of rodeo to the public. Be sure to watch the news for weeks and even months leading up to the interview. Reading a newspaper is also a good study source. Many judges will ask questions about current events.

When preparing for the private interview, know the local and national sponsors. Know what is going on in the news again locally and nationally. You should dress in a western suit or a more professional way. Remember you are applying for a job.

You might also practice for the interview by asking a friend who works in the business community and see if they will practice with you, as if you were applying for a job with them.

You have studied with your equine vet, you studied the PRCA rule book or the rule book of your rodeo association. You have studied the livestock welfare information. You know the names of your mayor and governor. You'd be surprised how many people get nervous and even forget the name of the President! Have someone drill you over and over, until it's second nature. This way, when you go for your interview, you will be very comfortable. This is also where your dance lessons will come in handy. You should not come schlepping in with your shoulders down like "oh, here I am," kind of an attitude. You need to go in with a straight back, just like riding.

Some queen directors advise shaking hands at the beginning and some directors advise shaking hands when they are finished. Find out at the competition what the judges prefer. You can ask your queen director to ask the judges.

Some things the judges look for and judge on are: How you are dressed, how you enter the room, how you sit down, and how you sit. They will judge your demeanor, whether or not you are nervous, or fidgety, if you are playing with the fringe on your jacket. They also note if you are calm, confident but not arrogant, if your voice is audible and not squeaky or tight. When the interview is over you need to rise gracefully from the chair, thank them for their time, leave and softly close the door. If you slam the door and say loudly "Gee, I'm glad that's over", the judges might hear and you will have lost many points toward getting the job.

This will also show the judges you might have two different personalities.

You are applying for a job of public relations officer for your hometown rodeo. This is a job interview. It is not how charming you are, what a lovely smile you have, or what pretty eyes you have. When you apply for a job with a corporation, they like it when you have done research about their corporation and that is why you have to study, study, and study some more. Know the rodeo terminology, rodeo expressions, history of each event, and why we have it. It is a living part of our American history. It's the past, still enacting in the future, with some modifications, such as more money for the cowboys. They can actually make a living now! It isn't simply one cowboy trying to beat another one. There is a tremendous amount of comradery among the guys. They will talk about how this steer runs, how a certain calf runs, how the horse is going to act in the chute, is he going to rear when the gate opens, is he going to take two runs and then start bucking. The cowboys talk about all of the little intricacies about the animal.

When you are studying, and can't find the information, go ask a contestant. If you live in an area where there are ranches, you can go to the rancher and say "I need some help. I am planning to run for rodeo queen and I need to know why we have team roping in rodeo?" "Why do we have calf roping?" Know which events actually came from ranch work and which events just came from cowboys bragging and having fun.

Before you go in, take a deep breath and let it out slowly. Shake your arms and legs. This helps to calm your nerves. When you breathe deep it oxygenates the brain. This will help your brain to think more clearly and also helps your muscles.

Another thing that needs to be addressed is awkward situations. Sometimes the judges will put the chair in the far corner and you have no place to sit, so what are you going to do? The only logical thing you can do, you ask the judges, "would you mind if I move the chair closer to you?" Wait for their answer, and then move the chair so it faces the judge's table but not too close, making sure you face the judges. To sit gracefully, face the judges and slowly back up until the back of your leg touches the seat of your chair. Don't sit to the side of the chair. When you sit down, do it slowly, don't plop. Sit to the front of the chair, have your ankles crossed and very calmly lay your hands on your lap.

I found by observation that sitting with one foot slightly behind the other or sitting with your ankles crossed and legs moved slightly to the left or right, is most attractive. Sitting with your feet together looks uncomfortable and soon your legs will separate and will look bowlegged. It is the little things that make or break the interview. For example: "Yep, I sure would like ta have this here job" or "Yes, I feel I am well qualified for this job".

At these interviews the judges are going to ask you about current events, rodeo, everything but personal questions. Personal questions are inappropriate. They should not ask you if you have a boyfriend, do you plan to get married and how many children do you want to have. No, no, no. If someone asks you a question that you feel very uncomfortable about, simply state, "According to the rulebook that my queen director gave me, I don't believe these topics were listed." You don't insult anyone but you are firm about it.

When a judge is asking you a question, look directly at the judge. Pay attention to the question. If there's some part of it you really don't understand, say so. Don't bluff your way through it. It may be a trick question. You don't know that, so ask them to please repeat the part that you don't understand. If you don't know the answer, be honest and move on. When you answer the question, look at the person who gave it to you and then look at the other judges. It is best to keep your answers simple and direct. Don't elaborate but don't give one word answers. Also, don't go off track and start talking about another subject. You will have just lost that question completely. Whereas, in the beginning you had the answer absolutely correct.

When dealing with controversial issues, never try to put your personal opinions off on the judges. You can sidestep strong opinions by being knowledgeable and talk about the facts surrounding the issue, while not stating a strong opinion. The judges are looking for the contestant who is able to handle these issues without offending anyone.

You should study the history of rodeo. Don't be intimidated by those who feel that rodeo is cruel to animals. The judges know it is not and you should know this also. Don't make up your mind that certain events are hard on the animal. They have a reason for it, know that reason.

Always look and act professional. Look as if you were applying for a job. Your makeup should be more subdued than any time in the pageant. Clothing should be more subdued also. This will allow the judges to concentrate on you. Make sure your outfit is comfortable and is a reflection of your personality.

Self-confidence is the key to any successful interview. Remember, confidence is attractive, aggression is a turnoff. Express your goals with pride but don't brag on an accomplishment and be humble. The judges know your accomplishments from your application. Do you know who you are and what you want to do with your life? Do you know what you can do for your town and for rodeo as a western sport? Can you express these confidently? If so, you will appear to have a good measure of self-confidence. This is usually what judges want to see. However, don't mistake being "cocky" for self-confidence. This will usually be a turn off to most judges while expressing yourself in a confident way will be received very positively. Be definite about your goals. Have a plan "A", if you win the title, and plan "B" if you lose the title.

You are going to have someone outside the room where the judges are. She is the timer. She is going to knock on the door and let the judges know they have one minute before they are finished with your interview. Then when she knocks again time is up, whether the judges have asked all the questions or not. Some contests have a silent woman in the room to make sure that all is fair. She may open the door as the contestant leaves the room. The judges will be given time to finish the scoring sheets on your interview. This person will tell the timer when the judges are ready for the next contestant. Most interviews have a ten minute time limit, but some can be shorter or longer, depending on how many contestants they have to interview in a certain time period.

Remember, you have studied super hard. You're going to know many of these questions. Just relax and don't be nervous. These are nice people. They don't want to bite your head off. Listen to the questions and answer them. If you knew all the answers and you finish before the ten minutes, you will be dismissed. You don't have to stay the full ten minutes. All you have to do is answer all the questions. If they ask you extra questions to fill the time, that would not be fair to the other contestants. If you finish in, say, eight minutes. Terrific! You knew it and you answered them well. Time is up and the judges will tell you that. The lady who is keeping the timer will introduce the next contestant. Pretty simple, don't sweat it. It will go okay. That's your last big hurdle.

To sum up, here are five attributes for a successful interview. They are enthusiasm, confidence, energy, rodeo knowledge, and knowledge of current events. If you have these attributes, you will have an easier time in the interview session.

I cannot emphasize enough that competitions can be won and lost in the private interviews so study, study, study. Make sure you know everything forwards and backwards. If the committee sends you a packet or notebook, read it. Have someone else read it so they can help quiz you. The judges will give you questions from that booklet and will expect you to know it. Don't use excuses like "this is too much to learn because I've been busy with school" or gymkhanas or busy with this activity or that activity. You were given the booklet. Study every single word of it. Someone put a lot of time and effort into making that packet and they expect you, in return, to study it. In fairness, the judges will ask contestants questions from that booklet, expecting you to have studied it. I can't emphasize this enough. You might have to give up some of your activities. Sorry, but there are only 24 hours in a day.

I had an occasion to visit a dear friend, Karie, who lives in Wyoming, she told me that she had run for a rodeo queen title. A few years later she applied for a job with AT&T. She used the above suggestions and she got the job. A couple of years later she applied for advancement and got the new job. She was paid a compliment on her interview skills! All the effort she put forth running for the rodeo queen title was well worth it. It isn't the title, it is the effort you put forth that will give you the skills you will need later in life.

"My shadow is small before the sun of your beauty".

Walking Drum by Louis L'Amore

Chapter 6

Modeling

This is the fun part in the pretty dress and all the glitter. It's a chance to show off all the hard work you've done. So where do you find proper clothes? Well, like I said before, if you've won the lottery you have no problem. But if you haven't, you borrow, especially if this is your first time. If you want to make it more yours, such as putting more sparkles on it, always check with the owner first.

When you do borrow, make sure it fits. As in horsemanship, make sure the sleeves come to the wrist and that the shoulder seam comes to your natural shoulder seem. Your dress should be smooth across the bust and tummy area and no lines across the hip area. A lovely dress, when it fits well, is a beautiful dress! If you wear a jacket, make sure the cuff comes to your wrist and you have room to move your arms freely when you model your ensemble. TIP: Most jackets look best when they come to your natural waste. If you have small hips, as most young girls do, then a peplum will give you the illusion of having some hips.

At one time a short dress came to one inch below the top of the boot cuff. Now a short western dress can come to the middle of the knee. So, the lesson learned is, Ask Your Queen Director what is the recommended length for short dresses!! Vests are inexpensive by comparison. However on most people they are most unflattering.

Color can be fun or frustrating. So many colors, what is a girl to do? Be colorized, it is so much fun. See your school's art teacher or better yet, according to my friend, Terry Rose, who had extensive training with Clinique, "go to a trained makeup artist for they will know what colors look best on you, and best of all, it is free. Use these colors as your color pallet for your clothing." Make a day of it. Have fun with it. Go to a fabric store and try to find the colors that were used at the makeup session. You can always ask for a small sample of the material and this might be free!

I love spring green. Can I wear it? No! Nor can I wear pink. I look as if I have the flu. They are just horrible next to my face. You might have the same problem with dark colors. They might darken your skin and make you look tired and worn out.

The same with dying your hair, you are young and beautiful just the way you are. Maybe a few highlights if you are older. You want colors that make you look vibrant. They should make your eyes sparkle, that makes you feel beautiful and comfortable. You can also go to the local dress shop and they might know how to help you select proper colors. If you have a junior college or community college, go there and see if they teach domestic engineering or clothing design. You can also go to the art department and bring some samples of material with you and lay them next to your face and have the teacher tell you if certain colors look good or maybe some colors will be terrible colors on you.

When we talked about horsemanship, we talked about sunscreen. At the start of the competition that is the one of the first things you put on so you don't look like a lobster the rest of the day!

As I've mentioned before, the organization I am most familiar with is the Miss Rodeo America. A couple of years ago, because my husband is a state judge, he went to their clinic to see what they are teaching the state queens, so he had a basis on how to judge them. One of the things they stressed was on how to cut down on costs was first buy your boots and your hat. Those can be the most expensive items that you purchase. A good felt hat should not be skimped on. It will show. Now, develop your wardrobe, especially if this is your first time out, around your boots and hat. Make your wardrobe interchangeable. Say if you are at a local level and you have to wear dark blue jeans and a white shirt for horsemanship you will be wearing black boots, a black hat and some silver earrings, really sharp looking ones. In many contests, equine interviews follow right after that. How are you going to change for that? You might not have a lot of time. You don't need another whole wardrobe for that. You can have a skirt that will go with everything. Just take off your jeans and put the skirt on with maybe a little bling belt and you're ready to go. Five minutes if you hustle. You can also leave your jeans on and wear an attractive jacket over everything. Make sure that the jacket comes to the waist. A long jacket can often make you look dumpy. If it's just a tailored, western jacket that comes just to the belt and then a pin or necklace that matches your earrings, you are ready for the private interviews.

Why am I talking about this when this is the chapter on modeling? Remember the word interchangeable. Some of the clothes used in horsemanship can be used in modeling, say the jacket. Change your earrings, wear a fancier skirt or maybe change your blouse and wear the same skirt. It's nice if the jacket has some color with it, like maybe roses or horseshoes on it. Those are fine and you can build on those colors. Maybe a red rose color, if pure red looks beautiful on you, with a black skirt and the bling belt. Do you see what I'm trying to say? Think way ahead of all the things you are going to have to do and how you can mix and match them. What about a dress you may ask? Great! Use the bling belt and the same boots and hat.

When you get to a higher level there will still be mixing and matching, but not quite as often. Read the packet you were given for the competition. See where the rehearsal is going to be for modeling, speech and impromptu questions. Are you going to walk out onto a stage or is it just a platform that has been built that has a step or two? Are you going to be in a theater where you come down an aisle? Will modeling be done during the dinner where you walk between the tables so people can see the dress? There are different opinions about modeling. I will give you mine. Modeling is to show off your personality, to show who you are. That means the line or cut of the garment you are wearing, the colors you are wearing, the fit of the garment that you are wearing, and the smile you are wearing, are all in western high fashion. It is a completely different genre. Do not separate your feet so far apart that you look like you're walking in a field. You want a smooth, even line. You don't want your head bobbing up and down as if you're just schlepping along. To me, modeling isn't just the smile of the girl; it's what I just mentioned, her choice of clothes for that particular portion of the competition, her gracefulness and how well she can put herself together.

Most commonly the order will be modeling, then speech, and then impromptu questions. Consider the design of the dress to complement your speech. Remember you will be on stage for a while. The judges are looking for the complete package.

Here are some suggestions from **Miss Rodeo America 2000 Brandy Dejon and Kayla Sperlock Duba, Miss Rodeo California 2005**. They stressed at their rodeo queen clinic, that while you are waiting for your turn to be on stage, to first stretch your arms, shake your arms, shake one leg, then shake the other leg. This helps to relieve stress. Stand tall and straight, take a deep breath and comfortably let it out. Oxygen feeds the brain and it feeds the muscles and it makes you more relaxed. What I do before I sing the National Anthem at rodeos is briefly close my eyes and see myself in the arena with passion and enthusiasm and sell my deep belief in my country. When it is your turn to appear on stage, stand tall and straight, take another deep breath and comfortably let it out. You should enter with a big, natural smile, glance slowly over the audience as if you were saying "hello" to each and every one.

Remember I told you about the note cards that you will need? For modeling you will write a note card which describes your outfit. Make sure you write two identical notecards. One for the emcee and the other is given to the person handling the music. The emcee and the music person will have a list of the order of appearance of each contestant. Realistically, unforeseen things do happen so to be on the safe side, have your name and the order number of your appearance on both cards. If you are to choose your own music, do the same thing.

Maybe your favorite song isn't appropriate for right now, like "Momma Don't Let Your Babies Grow up to be Cowboys." You are a cowgirl; now you are running for rodeo queen and supporting the cowboys and your rodeo association. Pick something that is a little more appropriate and walk in time to the music. It really bothers my eye when the music is quick and perky and you're just slowly gracefully moving down toward the stage. It's bothersome to the audience and it's bothersome to the judges. If you can walk in time with the music, please do. Some committees have their own music and the same piece of music is played for every single girl. You might think that is more fair, but one of the things the judges look for is personality. Personally, I like it when the girl chooses her own music.

I get a better insight into your unique personality, but I'm not going to be on the committee that makes these decisions nor will I be one of your judges. The point is, always check your packet first. If necessary, check with your pageant director or queen director to be sure, and never assume you know exactly what they want. Every competition is different.

Now it's your time to shine. Your mom has worked with you and now it's all up to you. All she can do is sit in the audience and be very proud of you. If you are modeling when they have a dinner, you will probably come from the back of the room and walk among the tables. Keep your feet slightly close together. Most people are right handed so you are going to lead on the right foot. This is for when you come from the back of the theater or the back of the room or when you are modeling between the tables. While you are modeling and the music is playing, the emcee will be reading your note card with a little bit about you and what you will be wearing, where the jewelry came from, such as who sponsored it or who is the designer. Never forget to name your dress designer. You should preferably use hats and boots that are made by your national rodeo sponsors.

You should make your notecard clear, simple and concise. When they are talking about the earrings and necklace and you are at a table, just gently move your hair back so you can show the earrings. Smile at the audience or the people at the table. Place your hand under the necklace, wiggle your fingers to give it more sparkle and luster. When you are walking keep your hands to your side. Keep an easy gait. You don't want to look stiff. That's where a ballet or dance teacher can come in handy. They can teach you how to move with the arms being in a natural, comfortable way. You need to keep smiling without having a painted still life smile. You need to practice in a mirror. It is modeling and you are showing how beautiful you are.

Oh dear, here are the dreaded steps. Everybody worries about it. Am I going to miss a step or fall? Am I going to step on the hemline of my dress? Two little secrets: first, if you're by yourself and you've reached the steps, take both hands and just slightly above the middle of your thighs, pinch the material and slightly lift it with the wrists being bent forward. It's a bit old fashioned but it is very ladylike. As you climb the stairs, you will also be turned slightly to the audience. You never want to turn your back to them or to the judges. Take your time and just go up to the top step to the stage. If you're fortunate enough to have an escort, he will take your arm, either lay it on top of his arm or he will wrap your arm around to where your hands are holding each other. Use him for stability. With your free hand, again, middle of the thigh, slightly pick up the skirt so you won't step on it. He will leave you on the top of the stage. You turn to him and thank him. You turn to the judges and acknowledge them by the nod of your head.

When it is your turn to model, take two steps forward and start your modeling. If you are fortunate enough to have a real theater and you have wings in the theater, the wings are those large pieces of material that hang down from ceiling to floor, there will be three or four of them. It is best not to come out on the first one. I would come out on the second one because it's just more attractive. When you start to enter the stage, you are coming out on the left side to the audience. You stride out first with the upstage leg. Upstage is the back of the stage, so you start out on your left leg. This way your back will not be turned to the audience. Then you move with your right leg. It is really very simple, as you will see during the rehearsal.

When you come out of the wings, if you have fringe on the dress, if you have a fish tail dress where it's full at the end, do a pivot or do something that makes it fly. If you have fringe on your arms, come striding out and turn slowly so that your arms look like butterfly wings. Do anything to show that you are starting now and to be slightly different. You walk across the stage with your arms swinging easily. I don't like straight arms. It looks too military. Be relaxed. Have the elbows slightly bent. If you're fortunate enough to have a runway, walk to the middle of the stage and use the runway. Walk down to the judges. Take one step back into the T position, or third position, and smile at the judges. If you are thin, a little narrow in the hips, you might have a lot of baroque or ribbons, or something that gives the illusion of hips. If you chose lots of detail in the hip area, turn sideways so they can see the detail of the dress. Then turn back and walk to the center of the stage. Turn again and walk to your right side of the stage, the left side for the audience. Pick someone out of the audience, not someone way back, but someone closer to the front, so you can smile at them and still see the stage and not accidentally walk off the stage. When you go to the end of the stage, remember to turn and stand comfortably for about two or three seconds. This gives you a chance to quietly take another deep breath. The down stage arm, the arm that is closes to the audience, is to your side with the elbow slightly bent. The upstage leg is now slightly bent. Your arm is now hanging down in a comfortable position. I like the upstage arm to come just slightly forward and touch the upstage leg so you look pleasant and comfortable. One trick, when you're standing, is to always put your weight on the back leg. You'll look a little more relaxed. Remember, if you are relaxed, the judges will be relaxed and the audience will be relaxed and you'll get that extra point.

When you reach the stage or platform, if there are steps and you have a long, straight skirt or dress on, make sure there is enough room for you to lift your leg to the next step. You don't want to hobble. Hobbling means that you have to turn sideways and your knees are together and you can only lift one foot and get it slightly up to the next step and push on your toes to get you up. It's very awkward. Yes, you can have a kick pleat. It's best to have it in the back of the dress. Never, ever have a kick pleat in the front of a dress. A side kick pleat might work but to be on the safe side put it in the back.

If you are wearing a long dress and black or brown boots, your hosiery should match the color of your boots. If you are wearing colored boots or a short dress, wear a natural tan one shade darker than your own skin color. If you have skin of color, try to match your skin color. The goal is a harmonious, pleasing to the eye, line.

Make sure there is no panty line. Always wear a bra. You might be very comfortable with a dress that has a built in bra. Nonsense! Every girl is a different size and shape. Put your own bra on. You don't want them Jiggling. I saw one lady who was such a lovely gal, great personality, but she was blessed by being well endowed. When she was modeling all you saw was all that jiggling. It looked like two puppy dogs in a gunnysack having a fight. It was most distracting. Good grief, you don't want that. How embarrassing! It is worth the money and the effort to go to a good lingerie shop. It will make your clothes fit better. It will give you more self-confidence. You can also find your hosiery there. You should buy panty hose to eliminate the panty line. When you are on the stage and you turn and walk back, the judges will see a line across the fanny, that's not good either. Panty hose are very important so you will just have to get used to them.

One thing I neglected to talk about was the neckline. You can have a mandarin neckline, a symmetric square, round, v, or an asymmetric, whatever flatters your face, but no cleavage. Remember, in the beginning, these are supposed to be young ladies of high moral standards.

You have to be highly critical when you are trying on clothes. Check the front, side and back to make sure there are no sagging areas, it's not too tight and no bare areas. You want to make sure it's not too short, where you have to alter it and completely change the style of the dress.

Sometimes we see the young woman barely take her eyes off the audience in the center of the room when they walk from one side to the other side of the stage. It makes her look robotic. When modeling, and this is only my opinion, I do not like to see them walk to the side and put their arm facing the audience on their hip. They throw the hip slightly out, then turn and walk to the other side of the stage, then throw the other hand on the hips so the elbows is pointing to the audience and point that hip. I find it very boring. My suggestion is to turn slightly toward the direction you are walking and pick out a friendly face and smile at them. Pivot and look at the entire audience, arms placed in a comfortable position or the upstage arm on the thigh so you and your dress are in full view. Repeat walking to the other side. If you have a jacket, remove it, fold it gently in the upstage arm and walk to the other side. This way they can see the entire ensemble. Turn slowly when you pivot, put the jacket back on, pause for a minute and smile at the audience.

Some of these dresses are $1,000.00 to $10,000.00, depending on how far you go up in rodeo queen competitions. The higher the level you go, the more expensive the dress. You want to show it off. This is modeling. If it fits you well, this is a beautiful dress. If there is fish tail on the back of the dress, turn and slowly walk back so they can see the beauty of the dress. If there is a lot of fringe on the dress, learn to turn so that the fringe flies. *TIP*: Use most of the stage. Think of it as an octagon and use all eight corners. How big of an octagon is up to you. Plot out your modeling accordingly.

No clunk, clunk, clunk because those stages will have an echo to them and they will resonate. Walk soft on the heel and put more weight on the toe. Come to the center of the stage. Again, if you have fringe on the bottom of your dress, or a fishtail or a bridal look, turn slowly for the bridal look but quickly for the fringe so it can fly. Then walk to the back of the stage, another quick turn, look at the judges, smile, your feet are in the T position. That acknowledges that you are finished with your modeling. Never, ever, put your fingers to the brim of the hat. That is a male gesture. A lady nods her head and a gentleman tips his hat. In lieu of completely removing their hat as they did in the Victorian days, they just touch two fingers to the brim of the hat. It's the same thing as recognizing a lady and you are now that lady. They saw you in horsemanship. They saw that you can be a cowgirl. Now they have to see that you can be a gracious lady.

"The virtue of all achievement is victory over oneself, those who know this victory, can never know defeat".

Lights from Many Lamps by A.J. Cronin

Chapter 7

SPEECH

So many young ladies dread the speech portion of the competition. Some, once on stage, panic and forget their speech. Some just stand there and cry and your heart just breaks for them. It's very scary to stand before a group of people all looking at you, waiting to hear a great speech, especially the judges, with pen in hand. The key to a good speech is research, research, research. I told you in the introduction just how proud I am of my state, Arizona. I mentioned that so you too should be just as proud of your state.

You need to find out about the history of your state. When it comes to research you can go on line, or to the library, or if your school is still teaching history and I've just been notified that some schools aren't, learn as much as possible about your great state. Go to the museums in your home town, as well as in the small towns in your state, go to the state capital. I'm sure they have a museum about your state. Find unusual facts. Make it different. Write all this down. You might think you're going to remember it but you're not. When you go to the museum you might find someone who was the first rancher or the first farmer in your state. You might say "I didn't know we became a state in 18 hundreds or 19 hundreds or whenever. Write it down, then you won't forget it. You might not even use it in your speech. It's just helpful to know.

Look through the packet you are given when you apply for a rodeo queen or teen queen position. It will tell you how long your speech needs to be and if you pick the subject or if the queen director and committee have picked the subject. Then you know what to research.

When you contact your queen director for the speech packet, ask her how big the stage is going to be and ask her about the microphone. Find out if it's cordless or does it have a cord. If you practice with a cordless microphone and you're handed a microphone with a cord, it's so easy to get tangled up and you don't want to trip or have to make circles to get out of that cord. I know I keep saying it but practice, practice, practice! This is the only way to learn, by repetition. Hold the microphone near your chin. Try to keep the mic as close as possible to the original position. This is to keep your voice from fading in and out. You have worked too hard for this to happen!

When you do a speech, pick no more than two subjects. Any more than that becomes confusing to the judges and you don't want them to get bored and lose the track of what you want to say. You're selling your state. You're selling your town; you're selling yourself as the perfect lady to win the title. It doesn't matter what level you are competing in. You are selling rodeo. You are selling the importance of rodeo. Remember, you are the public relations officer for a large corporation.

Once the research is done, now comes the time to write it. Put it in a chronological flowing form. When I am writing, I use a spell and grammar check. If I overuse a word it lets me know. It won't hurt to use that. You will be using several drafts. The first time you put it down is not going to be your final one. Why do I know this? I have gone through it. I was terrified when I had to speak at church. You write it, then you go over it and you go over it again and you change one word here and another word there. Now, there's a trick. Once you feel that you have it just the way you want it, print it out. Now, record it. You can start reading your speech to the recorder. Run it back and you can hear every bit of nerves, hesitation, mispronunciation, enunciation, all the mistakes are going to show. Don't get scared. It's only your first draft. Everybody gets scared at first. Do it again and do it over and over and over until everything is just the way you want it to sound.

First read it, and then slowly begin to memorize it. Then stand in front of a mirror and say the speech. Practice gesturing. Make sure you contact the queen director so you know how big the stage is where you will be giving your speech. Get painters tape, because it doesn't hurt the floor or tiles or carpeting, and just mark out the area so you know the area and can make your gestures fit the space.

Memorize, memorize and after you have it memorized, record it again. Are you reciting or are you talking? A good speech is when you are talking and explaining things, like the beauty of your state and the history of your state, the unusual things about your state. Video record it again. Record it while you stand in front of the mirror and practices gesturing. When you review it, you might say, "oh my, I really swung my arm out." or "I didn't move far enough to the left corner." or "I just sort of stood there, didn't I?" Nothing teaches better than a visual aid. It makes you more critical and more objective.

Once you have it memorized and you are comfortable, take the last video to an English teacher, a speech teacher and a drama teacher. Let them watch the video and critique it. Make sure you have a notebook, a pen or pencil to take notes down when they tell you what to correct. The teacher might find, in this spot you faded, you didn't pronounce this word correctly, you used this word incorrectly, and you need to emphasize this word more. Let them be your critics. Later on when you practice, have them come to a facility that you have acquired. Maybe your church has a stage, or a service organization.

One thing you might consider is taking ballet lessons. Have you ever observed yourself and your friends as you come home from school? You don't want to walk like that when you are presenting your speech on stage. Remember, it is poise, posture, grace and maturity. Dance instructions will help with posture and more graceful arm movements. All of this comes in when you give your speech. That's why it is so important to video record your practices. Let's say now you're ready. You have your speech right down to the last comma. You know it forwards and backwards. Try to start in the middle, then start at the end, so that nothing can bother you. You need to know that speech!

Okay, let's say you're at Kiwanis and they have a little stage. Get your tape out. You know how big that stage is going to be at the actual competition. If you can, invite the speech teacher, the english teacher and the drama teacher and even the ballet teacher. They can be the judges and they will sit in the first or third row, where ever they can see the best, with their pen and notebook in hand, just like the actual competition. Have your brothers, sisters, grandparents, friends, neighbors and sprinkle them throughout the room. Have someone cough. Have a cell phone go off. Have someone go out and come back in and let the door slam. Have someone talking to someone else and someone waiving across the room. All of this can happen when you are going to give your speech. People aren't quiet. You want them to listen to you but you know, things just happen that way and you don't want to let something distract you. That is why you practiced at home first, so no matter what happens, you can still go on with your speech.

You have practiced over and over. The ballet teacher will criticize how you come onto the stage, how you walk to that spot where you will be starting your speech. Some people call it the T position. Some people call it the third position and that's a ballet term. The right foot is pointed forward, ever so slightly to the right. The left foot, you bring the heel of the boot up to the arch of the right foot. Now you're standing and you have good posture. You smile at the judges and you smile at the audience. You make sure that the microphone is turned on, even if it's a karaoke machine that you bought at the toy store. It can be a microphone. It's going to scare you at first because you don't sound the same. Practice, one, two, three, a,b,c, Mary had a little lamb, whatever works for you. Practice with that, because the big room is going to be different than your bedroom, kitchen, living room, or wherever you practiced.

When you come out of the wings on the stage, those are the side curtains or when you go up the steps and you start walking, you lead with the up-stage foot. Up-stage means the back of the stage. So, if you are coming in and the audience is on your left side, you will lead with the right leg. This way your back won't be turned to the audience. Walk comfortably to your spot, and stand in the third or T position, with hips slightly relaxed. Your weight is mostly on the back leg. The emcee gives the microphone to you. Take the microphone, smile at the judges and smile at the audience, then take a slight step forward with that left foot, and proceed to give your speech.

When you are finished, you will step back to where you started. Never ever say thank you. Even though you have invited these people at practice, at the competition you have not invited the audience. They come because they want to support the program, they want to support their granddaughter, their friend, and they just wanted to come.

During a competition, it's modeling first, then speech, then impromptu questions. This is not a hard and fast rule. I have seen where impromptu questions are first, then the modeling, then the speech. Once again, read your packet. If it's not clear ask your queen director so there's no misunderstanding and you will not be flustered doing it in the wrong order.

You cannot get a good study time unless you watch and hear exactly what you are doing. If you decide to wear a dress with fringe on it, don't play with the fringe. Don't fuss with the buttons, don't play with the buckle. Simply stand there calmly. If you like, put one hand slightly in front near the belt and the other hand slightly on the side, both hands on the side, or clasp one hand on top of the other, palm to back of hand. Look relaxed. This is why you video record.

When your practice is over you talk to the teachers who have come to observe. Go over their notes and see what they suggest. They will have a copy of your speech. They might say go back to sentence so and so, you don't have to go back up on the stage. Just listen to their suggestions and try to recite it the way they say. The ballet teacher might say your arms were stiff, roll them back, and shake them a bit before you walk out on stage. Take a deep breath and slowly let it out. Waggle your hands, waggle your feet, anything that gets the nerves out, so that when you walk out onto that stage you're going to look calm, ready and happy to do what you have to do. Your ballet teacher can show you these little tricks and **don't forget to breathe**. So often you will be concentrating on your speech and moving here and moving this arm and smiling at that person. Speaking of smiling, pick someone out of the audience that has a friendly face and for part of the speech talk to them because the people around them will feel like you are talking directly to them. When you move to the middle or the other side, pick another friendly face and repeat the same process. When you are finished and you step back, keep your posture at all times, a nice straight back. It looks good, it shows off the dress and it makes you look terrific. I know this is an ideal situation but try to come close to it.

Most young girls that run for rodeo titles are an A personality. They love to achieve and they love to be active and you cannot expect to stop everything for this. You need to sit down and decide which activities you can eliminate until the competition. This is very important. You don't want to overdo and stress out and get tired. Remember, you have diet, endurance, horsemanship, speech to work on and research, people to invite to practices, go to the teachers and have them critique it and listen to it etc.

You need to video record every practice. Let's say you are the president of the school annual, involved in 4-H, do gymkhana and teach Sunday school. You just can't do all of that plus study, and do research, and run for queen. It is okay to have your mom or a friend help you get the information together so you can write your speech. They can recommend books at the library or on line. They can locate magazines with rodeo themes or western culture. They can help you gather the materials but it is important that YOU write the speech. Be sure to time the speech, being as close to the allowed length of time without going over. Some competitions have a bell that will go off when you reach the end of your allotted time.

After your reign, you may want to run for another title at another rodeo and eventually run for circuit queen. There are 12 circuits if you are with the PRCA. As I told you before, I don't know about Miss Rodeo USA and her competition and how you reach that level, so if that is your organization, make sure you know everything about it as I do about the PRCA.

As you run for higher, more important titles, like State Fair Queen, which in some states is just as important as being the state queen, some of the girls hire professional speech writers. Now, I'm giving you just my personal opinion. I feel that defeats the whole purpose of a rodeo queen program, in helping a young woman to grow and mature and face things that are difficult. It's nice to have someone who is an expert. Even the president of the United States has speech writers, but he has a very busy job. This is why you discuss which activities can be eliminated for a while, so that you can do it for yourself. It will give you a sense of self confidence and pride that you did it, you were able to stand up there and face people and give your thoughts about how you feel about your town, your county, your state and your country.

Remember the quote I gave you at the beginning of this chapter? "The virtue of all achievement is victory over oneself. Those who know this victory can never know defeat." If you don't win, you still conquered some things that might have scared you. I went to one competition where one young lady was terrified of her horse. It was her mother who wanted her to run. Please make sure you want to run for yourself and not for someone else!

Now you have your main speech finished and you think you are done with writing, but there is one more that you might have to write and that's your introductory speech. When you are first introduced, generally on the first day, they ask you to explain a little bit about who you are. It's one of the hardest things in the world, to write about yourself. Think about it; write it over and over again. Remember the unusual things about you. Were you the first girl at your middle school to be on the school football team? You want things that are maybe just a little bit unusual. Were you the president of the physics club? You don't see a lot of women in physics or in chemistry. How about barrel racing? Did you make the fastest run in a certain arena and the time still hasn't been broken. Think about this.

Maybe you have an unusual background. Are your parents from another country and now have their citizenship, talk about how proud you are to be first generation here and how important it was for them to learn the English language. You respect your heritage. Your introduction speech is usually one to one and a half minutes long. Check again with the queen director and see exactly what the time limit is and when you will be introducing yourself. Will it be at the meet and greet? That's where everybody is there, sponsors, competitors, family, friends, judges, important people from town, like the mayor and sheriff. You are brought up on stage and you are asked to announce who you are, your title if you have one, and a brief description about you.

Talk about the things you like, maybe you love to read, or raise rabbits, or have a ferret. Anything you think that would be light and pleasant and something just a little different and will stick in the judges minds. The little speech is the same as the big speech. First write it, memorize it, recite it, video record it, and then talk. Don't recite it as if you are methodically reading from a textbook.

At some Rodeo Queen competitions, now, you may find instead of a speech competition they have *extemporaneous speaking*. This is where all the contestants are in a privet room. One by one each contestant is called into another privet room and will draw one of 5 subjects from a hat, for example. They, the contestant, will read it, place it back into the hat, and will be given 10 minutes to compose a 1 ½ minute speech. When the 10 minutes are up the contestant will then be escorted to the stage and her name will be called by the emcee. The contestant will then walk on stage and present her 1 ½ minute speech. This is to see if she can speak publicly on a minutes notis.

The main thing to remember is to just talk to your judges and the audience. Just show your personality and shine!

"Twenty years is a long time. A man remembers a Woman, a fight, perhaps a good horse for twenty Years but not much else."

Treasure Mountain by Louis L'Amour

Chapter 8

Impromptu

The impromptu portion of a competition shows your ability to think fast. You are asked questions that can cover pretty much anything. It can cover your knowledge in areas such as equine, tack, rodeo events, rodeo history, local, state or national information, or current events. They can be serious questions about topics important to young people or fun questions, such as your favorite flavor of ice cream and why.

Impromptu often follows the speech portion of the competition. Generally, there will be two jars or two hats with questions in each one. One might be serious and one might be lite. You draw your serious question first, read it, and then pass it to the emcee. They will read it to the audience. This will give you a few seconds to think about the answer. They will hand you the mic and then you start speaking. Don't hesitate too long. It will make you nervous and it will make the judges nervous. You want to show that you know the answer. Remember, don't use the verbal garbage when answering the questions and don't over answer. Make it simple, clear and concise. By over answering you can dig yourself into a hole and won't be able to get out. Then, there goes some more points!

When you are done hand the microphone back, then you get to draw your lite question. It can be anything. What is your favorite candy bar and why? What's your favorite color and why? Besides cats, dogs and horses, what is your favorite animal and why? What is the funniest thing that has ever happened to you? What is your most embarrassing moment? They can ask any of this and you need to be prepared. Write these down, anything you can think of. See how you answer them and, again, video record, video record, video record. A good idea is to visit a pageant or two and take notes.

So here we go again. Practice at home. You need to know that rule book of your rodeo association. You should write them on note cards. You can also get them on line. There are web sites for this. You can take some of those questions and put them on your note cards. Practice, practice, practice. Are you getting a bit irritated by now with the repetition of the word practice? I'm the writer and I am! As I said before, repetition really does work.

After you have answered both the serious question and the light question, you nod to the emcee, return the mic and smile. Never thank anyone! Turn to the judges and smile at them as you walk back to the center of the stage. Acknowledge your judges with a nod, and then walk off the stage. Leave on the same side you entered and from the same wing that you entered.

TIP: If you don't have an answer, don't just stand there and say I don't know. Make lite of it saying something like, "I really did study. Somehow this question wasn't on the list of the thousands of things I did study!"

Asking former rodeo royalty what questions they were asked would be a good way for you to practice some answers.

Sometimes you are not asked a question but asked something like "give us a 30 second commercial for your rodeo". Some are questions that ask your opinion, for example "What do you think is the biggest problem facing teens today?"

Be careful not to reveal too much personal information. One contestant was asked "What is your most embarrassing moment?" The judges then criticized her when she revealed that her embarrassing moment had to do with finding a restroom.

Here are a few of the questions I have heard asked during the impromptu portion:

Who is someone you admire and why?

If you could be a superhero, who would you be and why?

Who are your local rodeo sponsors? (Make sure you don't get these confused with the national rodeo sponsors).

What is your favorite rodeo event and why?

What is a lap and tap?

Where is the PRCA headquarters?

What is the name of the horse in front of the PRCA headquarters? Who is on the horse?

How many rodeo events are there? Name them.

How many feet between the barrels in barrel racing?

Where is the Miss Rodeo America pageant held and when is it held?

Who is the current Miss Rodeo America?

Who is the governor of your State? (Also Mayor, Vice President)

If you had a million dollars, what would you do with it?

What can you tell us about the history of the PRCA?

What is the penalty for breaking the barrier in calf roping?

What was steer wrestling called originally?

Name five (or more) national rodeo sponsors.

How many circutts are there? Name them.

This also applies to the IPRA.

",,,,she is not to dream about, my friend, she is the dream.

Sakett Land **by Louis L'Amour**

CHAPTER 9

ETIQUETTE

Etiquette is sprinkled throughout the book. We talked about when you arrive at the rodeo whether or not you send a thank you note. Go back to the table of contents, find the word or the glossary and you will get the proper definition of the word. This chapter is titled Etiquette for awkward, uncomfortable situations that you might encounter.

Say you are at a rodeo social for your rodeo committee. There is a lot of alcohol and you're not allowed to drink. If someone comes up to you a little tipsy or even really drunk and they want to buy you a drink; you say "thank you but I can't. I'm in crown and banner." They say, "Oh, one little drink isn't going to bother you. Come on, let me buy you a drink." He might try to put his arm around your shoulder. You gently turn away and say, "I really can't but it's nice of you to offer. I see someone across the way that I really need to talk to," and get out of there. If you are thirsty, have a friend go the bar and get you a club soda with a twist of lemon or lime. Now you have something in your hand, something to drink, and you might be less likely to be bothered by a drunken cowboy or committee person wanting to buy you a drink.

If you are approached by someone who is a just plain rude or crude, and asked for personal favors, you are not obligated to do any of that. You might have your mother or another female friend nearby. You simply say to the cowboy, "excuse me, I need to speak with this lady" and you go to her. You tell her about the improper proposal. Then you go to your queen director. If it's another town, you go to that queen director for that rodeo and tell her who did it and what they said, no matter how embarrassing it is. You are not obligated to do anything you are uncomfortable doing. Remember, in the beginning of the book, I said you are to be a gracious lady of high moral standards. It doesn't matter what you did in your personal life prior, but it certainly matters when you are in crown and banner. You simply don't do it. It's not your responsibility; it does not come with your crown. Regardless of what some mothers think, you don't do it and I'm sure your mother will not allow it. She loves you and she doesn't want you to go through a situation where you are uncomfortable. So remember, improper proposals and drinks, tells you to get away from that person as politely as you can. Go to the queen director of that rodeo, whether it's yours or a visiting rodeo, take your mother with you and explain what happened.

If you're visiting another rodeo, after you speak to the local queen director, you call yours and you let her know what was done, how you handled it, what were the suggestions from the local queen director and what were her actions. Your queen director needs to know these things so that your life and your mother's life can be a lot more pleasant.

Well mom and daughter, you've gone through a lot. Don't try to absorb all of it at once. Just take it chapter by chapter and work with it. It can be really a fun time, and as I said in the introduction, it doesn't have to be a mom. I've seen a dad do this more than one time. Also grandmothers, aunts, uncles, girl-friends, a teacher, another adult, it doesn't have to be a mother if you don't have a mother in your life. The word mother is used as a generic term.

Another area of etiquette that has not been discussed is the announcers. It would help them tremendously because they have so much paperwork to do, if you can put on a note card, or your autograph sheet, your name, title and what area you represent. That gives them the basic information to announce you in the grand entry. If you're visiting from out of state, then list your state. Give it to the announcer at least two hours before the grand entry. He needs this time to be able to review everything and put it in order. If you have an unusual name, write it out phonetically, so he can pronounce your name or the name of your town correctly. He would be most appreciative. If he says your name right, go up to him after the rodeo and say "Thank you, it was such a pleasure to have you say my name correctly. Usually people call me so and so." It's just a little bit of kindness but it goes a long way.

Promptness is essential in rodeo. You can't come late. If you do, you're out. Rodeo demands that you are prompt. You have a huge audience. If you go to a concert, are you going to sit there and wait thirty minutes for it to start? I don't think so. If they say it starts at 8:00, it starts at 8:00. They give you a time and they start on time so make sure you are there at least two hours ahead so you can check in and give your card to the announcer. If you feel it is necessary, you can give a few points of interest, in case there are just two or three queens and he needs to kill some time, then he can read a few of your accomplishments, but don't expect him to do that. Usually it will be your name, title and where your rodeo is.

Be sure you are ready for the grand entry at least 30 minutes before the start of the rodeo. Make sure that you have your autograph sheets on time and that you have a marker that isn't dried out. You are the one out front. Your mom can stand back, keep a close eye on you and if she sees anything that in her estimation is improper, you can either step out and she can speak to the guy and say, " My daughter needs to circulate." or you can go to the queen director and ask what should be done.

Remember, this is a competition of knowledge, ability to speak well about rodeo to the public, good horsemanship, self-control, not getting upset when things get stressful, and staying focused on the task at hand. You should shine with confidence. Let your inner beauty radiate. The glittery clothes only enhance your true self.

You will be under a lot of scrutiny. If you are bossy, pushy or loud, they are not going to want to work with you. It is going to make it pretty hard for you. Regrettably, that is the reality of things.

Whether you are running for a title or when you have a title, go up and shake hands with the Dodge rep or the Coca Cola rep and say "Hi, I'm Suzy Q, I'm glad you're here at the rodeo. I'm here because I'm running for my hometown rodeo queen. This is so exciting. I hope you can come to my rodeo." Just chat with them, talk to them, and be friendly.

Remember this: absolutely every community is a small community and word gets around really fast about who is indifferent, who is arrogant, and who is warm and open and friendly. Even if you don't have a title yet, you could take a picture of the new Dodge and chat with the Dodge rep. You can ask if you could take a picture of you, the Dodge rep., and the new Dodge because they have made some changes. They are a very important sponsor. If there is Wrangler rep. there, take a picture with him. Say "Do you mind if I take a picture with you? I'd like to put it in my scrap book because I'm running for my local rodeo or state rodeo title and this would show that I'm really interested and I truly want the title." The same goes with the Coca Cola representative. Get out there and talk to people. *Everything is a small world.*

Speaking of a small world, improper conduct, such as throwing a fit if they give you the horse that you don't want, is always noticed. Don't be upset if you don't get the best seat just because you will be running for your hometown position. Dress properly when you get there. Don't come in shorts and t-shirts. I know they are comfortable in the summer when it's 100 degrees and the humidity is high, the clouds are coming in, but wear your Wranglers. Wear a nice shirt. You don't have to be overdressed, but just look properly dressed.

You, young lady are a liaison between the rodeo and the community. You must act properly at all times.

> "Take care of your horse and your horse will take care of you."

> **Anonymous**

Chapter 10

Equine Knowledge and Horse Care

There are three basic classifications of horses and about 100 breeds.

The common measurement of stature in the United States is the hand, which is four inches. If a horse is said to stand 10.2 hands, that means it is 40 inches plus 2 inches tall at the withers (the highest point over the shoulders when the head is down to graze).

A pony stands 10 to 14.2 hands and weighs 300 to 850 pounds. A light horse stands 14.2 to 17 hands and weighs 800 to 1,300 pounds. A draft horse stands 15.2 to 19 hands and weighs 1,500 to 2,600 pounds.

Ponies are generally defined as small horses and the development of the various pony breeds have been due to breeding for a specific purpose, such as working in mines or to customary or natural selection for smallness over a long period of time in a given area where a reduction in size was in better accord with the limited available food supply or climatic conditions. The best known breed is probably the Shetland pony, one of the smallest of horses. Light horses are used for riding, racing, pulling light vehicles, ranch work and warfare. The Arabian is one of the oldest light horse breeds and has contributed to the foundation of many others. In the United States, three breeds of light horse, the thoroughbred, standardbred and quarter horse, are used in professional racing as well as for pleasure riding. Draft horses were and are used for pulling heavy loads and for farm labor. Their numbers have decreased but they have a proud history. Among the better known draft breeds are the Percheron, Belgian, Shire and Clydesdale.

The common gaits are the walk, trot, pace and gallop. Thoroughbreds and quarter horses race at the gallop and achieve speeds up to 40 mph under loads (jockey and saddle) of 120 to 140 pounds. Standardbreds race at the trot and achieve speeds up to 33 mph. pulling a sulky.

Anatomy: In the adult horse, five years of age, there are 40 to 42 teeth, including 12 incisors, a large space occupied in part by the four small canines (often absent in the female) and 24 cheek teeth. The first upper premolar on each side, called the "wolf tooth" is very small and is frequently lacking.

The horse's digestive system is developed to handle forage. Unlike those of cud-chewing animals, the stomach is relatively small, holding 2 to 2.5 gallons in an adult light horse. The small intestine is 60 to 70 feet long but the large intestine is enormous and particularly adapted for digesting grass and hay. The circulatory, respiratory, endocrine, nervous and excretory systems are typical for a mammal.

The mare is seasonally polyestrous with most mares undergoing 21 day estrous cycles from March or April through September or October. The mare is in estrus (heat) an average of six or seven days each 21 day cycle. Gestation is an average of 338 days with a range of 325 to 400 days. Usually a single foal is born. When twins are conceived, one is usually resorbed early in gestation or both are aborted in mid to late gestation. Live, viable twins are unusual but not unknown. Foals are weaned naturally around six months of age. Domestic foals are weaned as early as three or four months. The life span is 20 to 30 years and in extreme case, up to 40 years.

Coat and Coat Markings:

The horse's skin is thin, and its hair reasonably uniform except for the long, coarse hairs of the mane, which springs from the upper border of the neck and adjacent part of the withers, and the tail. The fetlock, above the hoof, is so named because of the tuft of hairs on its rear surface. The hairs are more developed in the draft breeds and are called feathers.

The basic colors of horses are Bay, Chestnut or Sorrel, Brown, Black, Dun, Buckskin, Palomino, Gray, White, Roan, and Pinto or Paint.

White facial markings are stars, stripes, blazes, and snips. White leg markings are stockings and socks.

Vitals: The normal temperature of a horse is 99.5 to 101 degrees. The heart rate in an adult horse at rest should be 36 to 48 beats per minute. Respirations for an adult horse at rest are 12 to 24 breaths per minute.

Contributor: Dr. Carol Richardson, DVM

In preface let me say these are merely guidelines to study. It is impossible to put a lifetime of equine veterinary medicine into a handbook, but I feel those of us privileged enough to share our lives with horses need to be knowledgeable of their basic needs.

NUTRITION:

First, horses are mammals like us, they need feed, water and shelter. ***Basic rules:*** If you wouldn't drink the water neither should your four legged friend. Water consumption is based on work load and weather, for the most part. The hotter and or more humid the weather the more you and your horse sweat. (heat index) Therefore, the more water the horse needs to drink. Ten gallons is minimal consumption in cool weather in a pasture environment. High temperatures and fast work can push water consumption up to 40 gallons per horse per day. Guys, this is eight – five gallon buckets a day. Water your horse while he's tied to the trailer. Offer him water if there's a trough near the wash racks or warm up arena, refill his bucket as often as it's empty. The only time to limit water is if the horse is really hot, then wash him off, cool him off and then water him.

Horses are herbivores, by nature grazers. They would eat little amounts all day in a perfect world. For our convenience we feed them baled hay or pellets twice a day. This is fine for most of them; however, some horses have higher metabolisms and burn more calories thus needing more feed.

Food for animals is referred to as feed. Feed can be broken into three basic categories. Forages which are: hays, pasture, and pellets.

Grains: mostly corn, oats, wheat, and barley. Many are manufactured in mixed quantities to balance the ration. Corn is very calorie dense but deficient in lysine. Oats are nutritious but only have half the calories of the same weight in corn and horses are unable to process the hulls so oats must be steamed cracked or rolled for the horse to access the calories, barley is much like oats. Wheat is generally seen as wheat bran, a processed flake which provides a great source of phosphorus for horses on alfalfa hays. Rice bran hulls: what's left after processing ride kernels has a good source of oils that is good for providing fat soluble vitamins and omega fatty acids for hair condition.

The third category is supplements which provide vitamins, minerals, fats, and nutriceuticals like glucosamines, chondroitin, hyaluronic acid, yucca, psyllium, and MSM. Supplements are just that, they add to the diet and are used to balance the ration.

Many are toxic if fed in excess, so you need to work with a veterinarian or nutritionist if you are going to mix supplements.

Work/riding is rated in hours of exercise. One hour of walk, jog is light work. Two hours of riding at all three gaits medium work and three to four hours is considered hard work. The average horse in light work needs two flakes of alfalfa hay a day, medium work three flakes a day and hard work four flakes of alfalfa hay or three flakes plus three to five pounds of grain. Since hay is salt deficient, horses should have free choice access to trace mineralized salt. Grass hay is generally less calorie dense than timothy, clover, and alfalfa hay so needs to be fed at a higher rate. Average horse in light to medium work will need three to four flakes of grass hay a day plus grain to vitamin mineral balance. Hard working horses can generally not eat enough grass hay to maintain their weight. The average horse can only eat 2.5% of his body weight in feed per day. This means the average horse eats 25 pounds of feed per day.

Electrolyte supplements are beneficial if the weather is hot and humid and the horses are working hard. Electrolytes are potassium and sodium and chloride needed to keep the body's pH at 7.4. Sweating loses sodium and needs to be replaced with sale (sodium chloride). Potassium is needed for muscle contraction. Failure to use potassium correctly results in muscle tremors (Impressive syndrome or HYPP). Horses actually crave salt and will go to look for it as needed. If horses are provided enough water they cannot overeat salt. All horses should have salt available to them free choice all the time.

Joint supplements are highly recommended in speed horses to protect the cartilage from excessive wear and tear. They come in many forms. The primary ingredients are glucosamine, chondroitin, hyaluronic acid, all of which are normally found in joint fluid. Most supplements also contain vitamin C, manganese, and MSM (monosulfonic methane).

Hoof supplements contain primarily B vitamins and sulfur containing amino acids to promote healthy hoof and hair growth. B vitamins help stamina and appetite. These are usually found in sufficient quantity in good feed. Biotin is used to promote healthy hoof growth. In high doses vitamins can be used to calm some horses and are sold in products like Bcalm.

Fatty acids promote healthy coats and are found in oils, grains, and most popularly ride bran. Fatty acid is a source of fat soluble vitamins.

The average horse needs 10% protein in his diet, moderate working horses and early gestation mares need 12 to 14% protein, hardworking horses and late gestation mares need 14 to 18% protein rations.

Muscle development in horses is dependent on protein and exercise. As a rule, horses get fit faster than people and retain muscling three times longer than people. So if your horse needs to sprint three laps in the arena he needs to work three times a week for an hour or more. You can't be a track star watching TV all week. Your horse can't be a rodeo star lounging in his stall all week. Be sure to warm your horse up slowly so the muscles stretch and warm up. This prevents injuries. Just like human athletes you don't show up at the gym and take off sprinting. You stretch first. Horses are supreme athletes and they need balanced diets and conditioning to function at their best.

Minerals can be divided into two categories; macro and micro. The large quantity minerals (macro) are calcium and phosphorus which your horse needs to consume daily. Grass hay is generally low or deficient in calcium and thus requires supplementing. Alfalfa hay is low in phosphorus and very high in calcium. The ideal ration is two calcium to one phosphorus. Alfalfa is often 6Ca to 1 ph.

Micro minerals which need to be in the diet in small to miniature quantities Selenium needed for muscle strength, copper needed for bone and cartilage development as well as blood and enzymes. Iron is needed for hemoglobin to carry oxygen. Zinc and Magnesium mostly for muscles, manganese, chromium for glucose metabolism, sulfur for hooves and hair. Most micro minerals are toxic in large quantities. Be very careful when supplementing rations not to exceed recommended levels. Selenium in particular is toxic even in small quantities.

Vitamins are divided into two categories; fat soluble and water soluble. Fat soluble vitamin A,D,E & K are stored by the body. Water soluble vitamins B and C need to be consumed daily. Horses are capable of making their own vitamin D provided they have access to sunlight (ultra violet rays); Vitamin D is required for healthy bones. One of vitamin A's jobs is healthy skin, vitamin E has many jobs but immunity and fertility are probably the most significant. Vitamin K is required for blood to clot.

BASIC MAINTENANCE

In addition to feed, water and shelter, horses need vaccinations, deworming, grooming, and hoof care. The average horse needs groomed daily, certainly each time before and after you ride, his hooves trimmed every six weeks, dewormed every eight weeks, vaccinated twice a year and teeth floated as needed, averaging every two years. The American Association of Equine Practitioners recommends the following:

Vaccinations:

Annually: Rabies, Eastern and Western Encephalitis, West Nile Virus, and Tetanus. Influenza, up to every three months, depending on exposure. Rhino, annually for all sexes, 5, 7, and 9 months of gestation in pregnant mares.

Other vaccinations may not be optional depending on where you and your horse live.

Annually: Strangles, streptococcus equip, Botulism, Potomac Horse Fever, and Venezulan Encephalitis. Equine Viral Arteritis is used primarily in breeding farms.

Vaccinations for adult horses are generally divided into twice a year. *Spring shots:* boostering for diseases carried by mosquitoes and flies; Encephalitis and Tetanus, Fall shots boostering for cold weather diseases, Flu and Rhino. Your veterinarian can recommend the best season to booster for rabies and other vaccinations.

Deworming is the process whereby we try to kill the majority of the adult parasites in the horse. Horses are host to Tapeworms (Taenia equi), Bots (gastrophylus), Large Strongyles (Stronglyus edentates, S.equinus, and S. vulgaris), Small strongyles (Cylicostephanus, Cilicocylus, Cyathostomum, Tridontophorus, Cylicodontophorus and Gyalocephalus), Threadworms (Stronguloides westeri), Habronema, Roundworms (parascaris equorum), and Pinworms (Oxyuris equi). Each parasite has its' own lifecycle and drug sensitivity. As a rule, larval forms of parasites are not liked by our deworming efforts. Partly because the larvae aren't in the guy and not all our wormers are absorbed into the blood stream.

Some Common Anthelmintics (Dewormers): Praziquantal, Ivermectin and moxidectin, Benzimidazoles and Pyrantel Palmate.

The best way to avoid immunity is to rotate anthelminitics, use as directed for the appropriate parasite and administer the appropriate amount for the weight of your horse. Underdosing doesn't kill parasites and increases risk of immunity. Overdosing causes potential toxicity and does not increase the efficacy of the product. Fecal floats are a simple test the veterinarian can perform to tell you if your horse has parasites and if it needs to be dewormed, which product will be the most effective.

FARRIER AND HORSE SHOES

The equine professional you are likely going to see the most of each year is the farrier, alias horseshoer. The average horse requires shoes every six weeks. The typical range is four to eight weeks. In my experience performance horses with normal feet will outgrow their shoes well before eight weeks. The old saying, "No foot, no horse" still remains true. The competency of your farrier is directly related to your horse's performance. Small changes in shoes or shoeing techniques can make the difference between walking and hobbling.

Shoeing is the process of applying metal to the bottom of a horse's foot. Shoes serve to protect the hoof wall from excessive abrasions, protect the tender sole from constant trauma, enhance traction and support the bony column of the horse's leg. Properly applied shoes can be used to treat or prevent a variety of lamenesses. Horseshoes come in a variety of sizes, not just circumference, but width and weight as well. The average horse wears an 0 (aught) or 1 up front and an 0 or 00 (double aught) in the rear. As a rule front hooves are longer front to back, being more oval than hind feet which tend to be rounder. It is not unusual for horses to wear different size shoes even on their front feet especially if they have had a hoof injury.

Okay, so how do you set about to find your horse's new best friend? How do you know if the farrier is any good? There are several associations that certify farriers so this is a good place to start. The most popular is AFA (American Farriers Association). A certified farrier has had to pass a test for competency and passed shoeing school. AFEC certifies farriers who can do corrective shoeing. As we review the various lamenesses and leg conditions of the horse, I hope you will begin to see what a valuable part the farrier plays in the horse's well-being and your ability to ride competitively. It is extremely important that you, your veterinarian, and your farrier are a team.

Hoof balance is the term used by veterinarians and farriers to describe the theoretical ideal shape of conformation of a given foot, the position of the hoof relative to the limb above, and the way that the foot should be trimmed.

The term "hoof balance" has been used to refer to geometric balance (symmetry of hoof shape) dynamic balance (flat landing on the hoof on a hard surface), three-dimensional balance, and natural balance. No method of "balancing the foot" will yield optimum foot conformation for every variation of equine conformation. Balancing the foot may yield very different foot shapes depending on your horse's conformation (such as toeing I or out or a club foot).

The foot should be evaluated, trimmed and/or shod in a consistent, reproducible manner that considers: The hoof-pastern axis (HPA); the center of articulation; and Heels extending to the base of the frog.

Becoming familiar with the three basic landmarks will enable the veterinarian and farrier to approach trimming the equine foot in an individual, standardized and repeatable manner. Another advantage of these landmarks is the creation of a technical language that can be used to discuss farriery between the professions, and it will form the written basis for reports and records.

LAMENESS/DISEASES OF THE LEGS

The majority of lameness issues in horses occur in the lower leg. Many will respond at least to some degree by therapeutic shoeing. A number of common equine lamenesses are arthritis related including ringbone, sidebones and bone spavin.

The following are in diseases and causes for lameness. Many are listed in the Glossary of this book: Navicular Disease, Laminitis, Thrush, Whiteline Disease, Sole Bruises, Sole Abscesses, Quarter Cracks, Sheared Heels, Coffin Bone Fractures, Sidebones, Ringbone, Suspensory desmitis, Sesamoiditis, Wind Puffs, Bowed Tendon, Splints, Carpitis, Carpal Chips, Shoe Boil, Sweeny; Capped Hock, Bog Spavin, Thoropins, Bone Spavin, Stringhalt, Upward Fixation of the Patellar, Stifles, Knocked Hip.

Insert image 3

Diagram of a horse

Glossary

Action – How a horse moves it's feet and legs.

Added money – the portion of the prize money that is put up by the rodeo to attract contestants to the rodeo for competition.

Adrenal glands – two small, flat organs located on the front of the kidneys. Secrete hormones directly into the blood stream.

Aged – a horse over 9 years of age.

Agistment – paying someone else to board your horse on their property.

Aids – the legs, hands, weight, and voice are used to cue a horse.

Alter – to geld a horse.

Appaloosa – a breed of horse characterized by spots, developed by the Nez Pearce Indians.

Arm jerker – a horse or bull that is really stout and bucks with the power to cause a great amount of pull on the contestant's arm.

Astrigent – drugs that cause contraction of infected areas, such as alum, zinc oxide, or sulfate.

Average – the contestant's points are combined from all go-rounds and the contestant with the highest total points wins the average.

Azoturia (Monday Morning Sickness) – severe, painful cramping of large muscle masses, resulting in discoloration of the urine with the byproducts of muscle destruction. Commonly triggered in fit horses that resume heavy exercise after a few days or rest without any reduction in grain ration. A severe form of "tying up".

Bail out – a horse that comes straight up on its hind legs when coming out of the chute, then begins to buck.

Bailing out – intentionally jumping off a bucking animal.

Bandy legs – a horse that is pigeon-toed on his hind feet with his hocks turned out.

Bar shoe – a horseshoe that is closed at the back. A bar shoe offers support to the frog and heel of the hoof.

Barrel – the area on a horse's body between the forearms and the loins (also called the trunk).

Barren mare – a mare that will not breed, usually due to some medical problem. Also called an infertile mare.

Barrier – the rope stretched across the front of the box that the contestant's horse comes out of. In the timed events, the stock is given a pre-determined head start. The amount of head start depends on the arena conditions and is called the score. A contestant who crosses the barrier before the stock gets 10 seconds added to his time.

Bars – Fleshy area between front and back teeth on either side of the horse's mouth.

Bay – deep reddish-brown colored horse. Has black mane, tail and legs.

Bearing rein – neck rein – rein pushed against neck indirection of turn.

Bedding – the material spread on the floor of stables.

Biotin – water-soluble vitamin of the B complex.

Bleeding – an old treatment whereby a pint or two of blood was taken from a horse to improve performance. Rarely used nowadays, though there is some thinking that the practice stimulates the erythropoietic system.

Blemish – any mark or deformity that diminishes the beauty of a horse, but does not affect usefulness.

Blinkers – eye shields fixed to a bridle to prevent a horse seeing sideways or backwards.

Blister – an agent rubbed into the skin to treat certain lamenesses. Depending on strength, blisters cause mild rubefacience through severe blistering and pain. Their aim is to convert a chronic condition into an acute one thereby stimulating healing, or so the theory goes. This now has been all but phased out.

Blood spavin – swelling of the vein usually below seat of the bog spavin.

Blooper – an animal with very little bucking ability that jumps and kicks or just runs around the arena

Blows up – an animal that runs out away from the chute before starting to buck.

Bone spavin – bony growth usually found on inside lower point of hock.

Bog spavin – irritation of the hock joint resulting in swelling of the joint.

Bomb proof – a horse that doesn't spook.

Bone Spavin – arthritis of the hock joint.

Boot the bull – a term used to mean a particular bull can be spurred. Bull riders are not required to spur their animals, and if they can, they earn extra points.

Bots – induce dental disease, stomach irritations and stomach ulcers.

Botulism – bacteria toxin that causes progressive muscle weakness and eventual paralysis. Shaker foal syndrome. Spread through the soil, wounds and in decaying organic matter.

Bowed Tendon – enlarged, stretched flexor tendons behind the cannon bones.

Box (loose box) – the same as a stable. Stall is also used, but usually means a more open stable in which horses are cross-tied at race meetings or equestrian events.

Brand – a mark or identification. A private registered mark burned on cheek, shoulder or hip. A number burned on upper neck of army horses. Can be tattooed inside of upper lip to avoid disfiguration.

Break-in – the education and training of a horse to accept a rider or be driven in harness.

Breaking the barrier – when a contestant rides through, or breaks the barrier before it is released.

Breaking the barrier adds a penalty of ten seconds to the contestant's time.

Broke – a horse that has been "gentled" to the point that he can be handled and ridden.

Bronc rein – a thick rope 1 ½ to 2 inches in diameter that is attached to the halter of a saddle bronc horse. The rope can be no longer than 6 ½ feet and is used to provide balance and to give the cowboy something to hold onto.

Broodmare – a female horse kept for breeding purposes, ultimately to produce and nurse foals.

Broom tail – a western range horse, a poor, ill kept horse of uncertain breed.

Buck – when a horse leaps into the air, keeping his forelegs stiff and his back arched, while lowering his head, sometimes kicking back in an effort to unseat a rider.

Buck kneed – knees bent forward.

Bufford – an animal that is easy to ride, ripe or throw down.

Bull rope – a flat woven rope, no larger than 9/16th of an inch in diameter with a bell attached to it. The rope is wrapped around the bull's body, just behind the front legs, and then around the cowboy's hand, to help secure the cowboy to the bull.

Bumpers – another name of the ergot region, usually of the hind legs in gallopers. A horse "getting down on the bumpers" is over-flexing the fetlocks allowing the ergot to contact the ground, which results in bruising.

Bursa – sac or cavity filled with fluid, located in a joint or other place where friction is likely to occur, provides lubrication between ligaments, tendons and the bones over which they run.

Bursitis – inflammation in a bursa that results in swelling because of extra synovial fluid.

Bute – Pheylbutazone. A medicine that is non-sterodial anti-inflammatory equivalent to aspirin.

By – if a horse is "by" a certain stallion, it means that stallion is the horse's sire.

Calf-kneed – opposite of buck kneed, knees bent backward.

Cantle – the extreme back of the saddle.

Cantle boarding – when the backward stroke of the legs of a saddle bronc rider's spurring motion reaches the saddle's cantle.

Capped Hock – irritation of the hock joint resulting in swelling at the top and back of the hock often related to trauma like stall kicking.

Carpal Chips – small bone fragments break off one or more of the eight bones making up the horse's knee. This is a traumatic injury most often caused by kicks, falling on knees or racing.

Carpitis – irritation of the knee (carpus) results from hard ground, poor conformation, poor shoeing, and inadequate conditioning.

Cartilage – specialized type of fibrous connective tissue covering bone ends at joints; also structural basis for ear, nostril, etc.

Cast – being cast in a stable means that the horse has rolled against the wall and cannot get up. A cast horse will struggle and kick to get away from the wall and can be injured in the process. Most horses learn not to get cast after the first few times.

Castrate (geld, cut) – to surgically remove the testicles of the male.

Cataract – cloudy or opaque appearance of the eye.

Catch as catch can – a calf roper is allowed to catch the stock any way he chooses so long as he turns loose of the rope when throwing the loop and so long as the rope holds the calf until the roper reaches it.

Cavesson – a noseband on a bridle. A stiff noseband on a halter used with lunge line in training.

Center fire – a western saddle with cinch hung from center.

Champion – the rodeo champion is traditionally the highest money winner in an event for the given season.

Chasing the cans – the rodeo nickname for barrel racing.

Chestnuts – the horny growths on the inside of a horse's legs.

Chute fighter – a rough stock animal that will not stand still and tries to fight the cowboy before he leaves the chute.

Coarse – lacking refinement.

Coffin bone – the bone inside the hoof closest to the ground, designated "P3".

Coffin joint – joint space between the coffin and pastern bones.

Coggins – test for EIA.

Cold-blooded – designating any horse or breed of horse without Arabian or eastern blood in its breeding.

Colic - #1 killer of horses. Signs include turning head toward the flank, kicking or biting at the abdomen, pawing, stretching out as if to urinate, repeatedly getting up and down, violently rolling, sitting in a dog like position, lack of bowel movement, lack of appetite, elevated pulse rate and sweating.

Collected – controlled gait, a correct coordinated action.

Colt – a male foal.

Condition – the horse's fitness and readiness to run. Body condition is essentially grading of muscle and fat content.

Conformation – structure, form and symmetrical arrangement of the parts of a horse.

Congenital – an abnormal condition that an animal possesses at birth such as a hernia.

Contracted feet – abnormal contraction of the heel.

Coon footed - long sloping pasterns throwing fetlocks low.

Corona – saddle pad cut to fit shape of saddle, has a large colorful roll around edge.

Coronet – the small area that attaches the hoof to the rest of the leg.

Corticosteroids – analogs of the hormone cortisol produced primarily by the adrenal glands. May be natural or synthetically produced for injection.

Coupling – region of the lumbar vertebrae, line or space between last rib and hip.

Cow-hocked – hocks close together, feet wide apart.

Cowkick – horses usually kick backwards but a few can kick out to the side like a cow.

Crest – upper, curved part of the neck, peculiar to stallions.

Cribbing (cribbiting) – biting or setting teeth against fence or other objects while sucking in air.

Cross-firing – a condition in which the hind foot hits or scuffs the inside front diagonal foot.

Croup – part of the back just in front of base of tail.

Crow hopping – mild bucking action.

Cut proud (proud cut) – geldings that act like stallions even to the point of trying to serve mares are referred to as being cut proud.

Cutting horse – a horse trained to separate, or cut out, one animal, usually a cow, from a herd.

D.V.M. – doctor of veterinary medicine.

Dally – a turn of the rope around the saddle horn after the animal has been caught.

Dam – female parent of a horse.

Dink – a turn of the rope around the saddle horn after the animal has been caught.

Dished – concave, referring to the profile of a head, such as that of an Arabian.

Dock – the area at the top of the horse's tail; also describes a surgical procedure to remove the tail.

Dog fall – an illegal fall in steer wrestling that causes the feet of the steer to be in a different direction than the head. To receive a time the cowboy must turn the steer over or let it up and throw it again with the hind legs, before the hind legs touch the ground.

Go round – when all contestants in an event have competed one time, it is called a go-round.

Goose -rumped – having narrow, drooping rump.

Go short – to take short steps, indicative of lameness.

Grabbing the apple – the term used when a saddle bronc rider touches any part of the saddle with their free hand during the eight second ride. This is also known as "pulling leather" and causes the rider to be disqualified.

Grade horse – a mixed breed of horse.

Gray – any color from pure white to dark gray.

Green horse – one with little training.

Groom – person who looks after the horse.

Ground money – the money paid when the purse for an event is split equally and paid to all contestants in the event. This is done when all contestants entered in an event fail to qualify.

Ground work – lead rope and lunge line training.

Hack – any horse used for normal riding, formal or informal. A hack event at a show is a formal competition for ridden horses judged on type, presentation and performance.

Hand – a measure of the height of horses; equals four inches.

Hard keeper – a horse whose weight is hard to maintain.

Harness – strictly speaking, any equipment used on horses to ride or drive them, but usually restricted to driving gear.

Hat Bender – a horse or bull that does not buck and just runs around the arena.

Haw – a third eyelid or membrane in front of eye, which removes foreign bodies from the eye.

Hazer – in the steer wrestling event, he is the cowboy that rides on the opposite side of the steer and keeps the stock running straight down the pen for the contestant.

Head collar – a British term for a halter.

Head hunter – a bull that is constantly looking for a two-legged target to hit.

Header – the cowboy that ropes the steer around the horns, head or neck in team roping.

Heaves – difficult breathing, lung damage.

Hock – the joint bending backward in a horse's hind legs; the hock is composed of the same bones as in your ankle, but the fetlock is commonly called the "ankle" because of its outward appearance.

Head thrower – a bull that tires to hit the cowboy with his head or horns while the contestant is on his back.

Heeler – the cowboy that ropes the hind legs of the steer in team roping.

High roller – the term used to describe a horse that leaps high into the air when bucking.

Hogged – short cut mane.

Honda – a ring of rope, rawhide or metal on a lasso through which the loop slides.

Honest bucker – an animal that bucks the same way every time out of the chute.

Honker – a really rank and hard animal to ride.

Hood – see blinkers

Hooey – the knot used by calf ropers to hold the wraps used to tie three of the stock's feet together after the calf has been thrown. This knot is known as a half hitch to most people outside of rodeo.

Hoof – horse's "feet".

Hooky – a bull that is really handy with its horns.

Horn or hoof wall – the material of the hoof. Horns can be pale, dark or mixed and all colors are similar in hardness.

Horn wrap – a leather device that is placed around a steer's horns in team roping to prevent damage to the steer's head.

Horse length – eight feet.

Hung up – a rider that is off the animal but is still stuck in the rigging or bull rope.

Hyperkalemic Periodic Paralysis (HYPP) – this is an inherited disease which will show through uncontrolled muscle twitching or profound muscle weakness. It can be maintained through diet and medication.

IFR – International Finals Rodeo.

In the well – the term used to describe when a contestant comes off an animal on the inside of the spin.

In work – a horse that is training for competition.

In season – when a mare is in heat.

Influenza – similar to a cold. Symptoms include fever, nasal discharge, and loss of appetite. It can be transmitted through nasal discharge, coughing and sharing of equipment, although it is not deadly. Vaccinate annually and if traveling, every 3-4 months.

Interfering – the striking of cannon, fetlock or pastern by the opposite foot front pair or back pair, that is in motion. This condition is predisposed in horses with base-narrow or toed out (splay-footed) stance.

I.P.R.A. – International Professional Rodeo Association.

Irons – colloquial expression for stirrups.

Ivermectin – generic name of an anti parasitic agent.

Jack – a male donkey or ass.

Jaquima – Spanish bridle or hackamore.

Jerk down – after roping the calf, the rope flips the calf straight over backwards.

Jockey – the leather flaps on the side of the saddle.

Jump and kicker – a bull or bronc that jumps and kicks its hind feet in a straightaway action.

Kack – the saddle used by saddle bronc riders.

Knocked Hip – refers to an injury of the hip which displaces the head of the femur from the socket. It is the result of severe trauma like a bad fall.

Lactic acid – by product of the breakdown of stored carbohydrates normally present in the body in small, harmless quantities. Occurs in excess where there is insufficient oxygen supply to the cells, especially muscle cells during strenuous exercise.

Lameness – a problem with the use of the foot or limb or limbs, due to athletic injury, trauma or disease.

Laminae – altering "leaves" of flesh and hoof horn that bond the wall of the hoof to the underlying bone.

Laminitis – a blood pressure related vasculitis of the sensitive laminae of the hoof wall.

Large Strongyles – also known as blood worms, can destroy arterial walls and blood vessels, impair the circulatory system and can cause brain damage and other disorders.

Lariat – from Spanish, la reata, meaning the rope.

Laminitis – disturbance of the sensitive plates or soft tissue, or laminae, in the horse's foot. Acute laminitis refers to a disturbance with rapid onset and brief duration, while chronic laminitis is persistent, long term disturbance. Either, in severe cases, may result in founder, and internal deformity of the hoof.

Lead – the first stride in the canter. When cantering or galloping, the foreleg that strikes the ground first is called the leading leg.

Legal catch – in team roping, the header must catch the steer around the horns, head, or neck. This is also called a fair catch.

Lens – transparent structure in the eye, lying behind the iris. Focuses light rays on the retina. The retina in turn transmits the light rays to the brain, where they are perceived as an image.

Level headed – a term to describe a horse that isn't excitable and is calm and quiet even in unfamiliar situations.

Lounger – a horse that thrusts with its hind feet forward rather than kicking out behind.

Lunge (longe) – to work a horse in a circle on the end of a long rope. Lunging is a convenient way of exercising horses. Continual working in a circle can predispose to leg problems such as splints. It can also make a horse sour.

Maiden – a maiden mare has not previously been to stud. A maiden eventer has not previously has a win in that event.

Mare – a female adult horse over the age of three years.

Mash up – a cowboy that clamps with his legs and has no spurring motion.

Measure the rein – used in saddle bronc riding. The length of the rein from the horse's head, in an upright position, to the rear of the well on the saddle. Then you measure from there depending on how much the horse drops its head while bucking.

Mecate – a hackamore lead rope.

Mellow hide – soft, pliable, and easy to handle.

Money horse – a horse that when ridden, usually takes the cowboy to the pay window.

Mount – to get on a horse. A stallion mounts a mare to service her. The horse itself may be referred to as a mount. Mounts on a saddle are the girth, surcingle, stirrup leathers and stirrups.

Mouth – to mouth a horse is to accustom it to a bit. Horses have a good mouth if they respond well to the bit.

Mucking out – removal of dirty bedding and replacing it with clean bedding.

Mugger – the cowboy who gets a firm hold on the animal's neck during the Wild Horse Race or Wild Cow Milking so that the horse can be saddled or a cow milked by his partner.

Mule – a cross between a jack and a mare.

NFR – National Finals Rodeo.

Navicular bone – small, boat shaped bone located behind the coffin joint in the hoof, regulates the angle at which the deep flexor tendon attaches to the coffin bone.

Navicular disease – most commonly found in high performance horses or horses with misalignment of the bones. Symptoms include short choppy strides and a tendency to land on the tow. The flexor tendon is more of the problem. If treated soon enough with corrective shoeing, horse has a good chance of recovering.

Near side – the left side of a horse.

Neat's foot - an oil made form suet, feet, and bones of cattle, used for softening leather.

Neck rope – a loose rope around a calf roping horse's neck through which the lariat is passed. It prevents the horse from turning away from the calf once it is caught and the roper has dismounted. Timed event cattle also wear a neck rope and it provides the means to give the calf or steer a head start. The rope is tied together with a piece of string and it breaks loose from the animal when the barrier is released.

No time – if no time is given to a contestant's run it means the stock was not properly caught, tied or thrown or a barrel racer has run off the pattern.

Off side – right side of a horse.

On the tow (toey, up on the tow) – these expressions mean the horse is eager to work or go faster. Toey horses chomp at the bit, take very collected steps and often prance and dance sideways (sidle) until they are allowed more rein.

Open behind – hocks far apart, feet close together.

Out of – if a horse is out of a certain mare, that means she is the dam of the horse.

Outfit – the equipment of a rancher or horseman.

Out the back door – when the rider is thrown over the back end of an animal.

Outlaw – a horse that cannot be broken.

P.B.R. – Professional Bull Riders.

P.R.C.A. – Professional Rodeo Cowboys Association.

Padding – throwing the front feet in an outward arc. Pigeon or toed-in horses will be in this category.

Paddock – a small enclosure adjacent to a barn, in which horses are turned out and can exercise.

Palamino – various shades of gold. Has a white mane and tail.

Parrot mouth – lower jaw is shorter than the upper jaw.

Passenger – a person who rides a horse without control.

Pastern – the region above the hoof but below the fetlock on a horse's leg.

Paunchy – too much belly.

Peggy Stride – short, quick step as a result of unsoundness in both front legs. Old horses with arthritis in front joints and old rope horses may exhibit this condition.

Pick up man – the cowboy on horseback who assists the bareback and saddle bronc riders in dismounting from their stock.

Piggin string – a small rope about six feet long used by calf and steer ropers to tie the animal's feet together.

Pin worms – irritate the horse's tail region and cause tail rubbing.

Pointing – standing with front leg extended more than normal – a sign of lameness.

Points – any animal will have its good and bad points. Points can also mean the extremities, usually used in reference to color – a bay horse has black points, meaning the mane, tail and legs from the hock and knee down are black. Points are also the conformational landmarks described under points of the horse.

Poll – the top of a horse's head, just back of the ears.

Polo chain – a chin chain of flat, large links.

Pommel – extreme front of saddle.

Pony – a horse under 14.2 hands.

Port – the part of the mouthpiece of a bit curving up over the tongue.

Potomac Horse Fever – cause of loss of appetite, fever, depression, diarrhea and/or laminitis. Transmitted by blood sucking insects.

Pounding – a condition in which there is heavy contact with the ground in contrast to the desired light, springy movement.

Producer – the individual that runs the rodeo and is responsible for bringing all the elements together into a fast, smooth running, and exciting production.

Pull leather – holding on to the saddle with hands while riding a bucking horse.

Purse – the money paid to the winners of each rodeo event. It equals the total of the added money and entry fees.

Quarter crack – vertical split in the wall of the hoof.

Quidding – dropping a bolus (quid) of partially chewed food from the mouth, usually an indicating of tooth problems.

Rabies – contracted by a bite from an infected animal. Vaccinate annually.

Rank – a very hard animal to ride.

Ray – a black line along the spine. Also called the dorsal stripe.

Rear – when a horse rises to stand on his hind legs.

Reata – Spanish for lasso.

Re-ride – another ride given to a saddle bronc, bareback bronc or bull rider in the same go-round when either the stock or the cowboy is not afforded a fair opportunity to show their best.

Re-run – a second run by a timed event contestant because a judge has ruled the contestant did not have a fair chance the first time.

Retina – sensory membrane lining the back surface of the eye's interior. The lens focuses an image onto the retina, which in turn transmits it to the optic nerve.

Rhino – a herpes virus that is airborne; causes spontaneous abortions and respiratory complications. Vaccinate annually/semi annually, 5, 7, 9 months of pregnant mares and every three months for foals.

Rig (cryptorchid) – a horse with only one visible testicle, the other being up inside the abdomen or inguinal canal.

Ringbone – bony growth on either or both sides of the pastern.

Rising – if a horse is rising a certain age it means the horse will be that age next official birthday. A horse rising five is a four year old.

Roached back – thin, sharp, arched back.

Roaring – difficult breathing due to obstruction, usually in the larynx.

Rodeo secretary – the person responsible for collecting entry fees, recording official times and scores, paying the contestants their winnings, and sending the headquarters office the results of the rodeo, as well as the sanctioning fees. Usually works as a timer too.

Rogue – a horse with a bad temper.

Rolling – side motion of the forehead. Excessive lateral shoulder motion, characteristic of horses with protruding shoulders.

Round worms – also known as Ascarids; can cause colic, heart damage, liver and lung damage.

Rowel – the circular, notched, bluntly pointed, and freewheeling part of a spur. Any competitor using spurs that will cause a cut is disqualified.

Run away – a horse or bull that does not buck and just runs around.

Sacking – so slap a horse with a sack, saddle blanket or tarpaulin as a part of breaking and training.

Saddle marks – white patches of hair usually in the wither region, an indication of pressure from an ill-fitting saddle.

Scalping – the coronet or hairline at the top of the hind foot is hit by the toe of the forefoot as it breaks over.

Scooter – an animal that pivots on the front feet and scoots the back end around instead of pivoting on the front feet and kicking the hind feet.

Seedy – atrophy or decrease in size of a single muscle or group of muscles, usually found in shoulder or hip.

Seeing daylight – term used when a cowboy comes loose from a bucking animal far enough for the spectators to see daylight between the cowboy and the animal. Also in tie down roping the calf's body must show daylight under its belly before being laid down.

Sesamoiditis – irritation of the sesamoid (pulley bones) in the back of the fetlock joint and is primarily seen in young horses and race horses.

Set you up – a horse or bull that drops a shoulder like they are going to turn or spin in one direction, and then immediately does the exact opposite.

Shankman – the cowboy in the Wild Horse Race that grabs and holds onto the lead line attached to the horse's halter so the mugger can get a hold on the horse's neck.

Sheared Heels – a defect in the heel of the foot where one heel is higher than the other. This can result from serious hoof / coronet injuries or improper shoeing where the foot is not balanced medially to laterally.

Shock – failure of the vital body systems, characterized by loss of blood volume and pressure, shallow breathing and rapid heartbeat. Usually the direct and potentially fatal byproduct of extremely serious injury, stress or illness.

Shoe boil – soft, flabby swelling at the point of the elbow.

Shy –act of taking fright at something and jumping sideways or backwards very suddenly.

Sickly hocked – with a curved, crooked hock.

Sidebones – an ossification of the collateral cartilage of the coffin bone. What should be flexible becomes bony.

Sire – the male parent of a horse.

Slab sided – flat ribbed.

Slinger – a bull that tries to hit the cowboy with his head or horns while the contestant is on his back.

Small Strongyles – cause inflammation of the intestines, resulting in weight loss and even anorexia.

Snaffle-key bit – a snaffle with small metal pieces dangling from center used in training colts.

Snorty – a bull that blows air at a clown or downed cowboy.

Sole Abscesses – pockets of drainage secondary to puncture wounds of the sole, severe bruises or incorrect showing putting pressure on the sole.

Sound – free from any abnormal deviation in structure or function, which interferes with the usefulness of the individual.

Speedy cutting – similar to cross-firing, this condition is involving a hind leg and the diagonal front leg. In speedy cutting however, the ankles or pasterns interfere.

Spell – this means giving a horse a rest, which may be at a spelling farm in the case of racehorses. A meaningful spell is anything from a fortnight to three months or even longer if recovering from an injury.

Spinner – a bull or bronc that comes out of the chute and spins to the left or right.

Splint – fracture of the slender bones (splint bones) in the cannon.

Spraying – inspection and/or prophylactic spraying for cattle ticks is carried out at a border or a designated tick treatment facility when moving horses interstate.

Spurring lick – a motion of the cowboy's feet.

Stall walking – a stable vice in which the horse paces endlessly around his stall.

Stallion – a male horse that hasn't been gelded.

Stargazer – a horse that holds his head too high.

Stifled – a generic term which refers to an injury of the stifle joint.

Stock contractor – the person or organization that provides all of the livestock used in the rodeo events.

Strangles – highly contagious infection of the lymph nodes, usually of the head, caused by Streptococcus equi bacteria. The abscesses may become so large as to obstruct the airway and may break internally, draining a creamy discharge through the nose.

Strike – a defensive lashing out with one or both forelimbs, which can be quite unexpected and very fast and cause serious injury to someone standing in front of the horse.

String bone – nervous disorder characterized by excessive jerking of the hind leg.

Stringhalt – a tendon problem of the hock/stifle (stay apparatus) which produces a goose-stepping gait behind. It responds to corrective shoeing.

Stud – a stallion used for breeding purposes.

Sucks back – an animal that bucks in one direction then instantly moves backward.

Sun Fisher – a bucking horse that twists his body in the air. A horse that bucks and all four feet stick out to the side instead of underneath or behind the animal.

Surcingle – a broad strap about the girth, to hold the blanket in place.

Suspensory Desmitis – an irritation of the tendons and ligaments that support the fetlock joint. Most common in running horses including barrel racers. Can be prevented by use of sports medicine boots.

Swap ends – an animal that jumps into the air and turns 180 degrees before touching the ground.

Sweeny – atrophy or decrease in size of a single muscle or group of muscles, usually found in shoulder or hip.

Symmetrical – proper balance or relationship of all parts.

Synovial fluid – stick, transparent lubrication fluid in joint cavities and tendon sheaths.

Tack – equipment used in riding, including the saddle, bridle and saddle pad.

Tapadera – stirrup cover.

Tape worms – may result in severe ulceration of the large intestine.

Tetanus (Lockjaw) – rigid paralytic disease caused by Clostridium tetani, a bacteria that lives in soil and feces.

Thoropins – irritation of the ock joint resulting in swelling that leaves a bump in the middle of the joint which can be pushed moving the fluid from the inside to the outside of the limb under pressure.

Throat latch – the under side of where a horse's jaw and neck meet. Also part of the bridle.

Thrush – a fungal infection of the sole / sulcus of the frog which causes a bad odor and/or pain. It is preventable by keeping the horse in dry conditions where his foot is not routinely damp, muddy or mucky.

Thorough pin – puffy swelling, which appears on upper part of hock and in front of the large tendon.

Tie down – a western term for a martingale, used to control the position of a horse's head while riding.

Timers – the persons responsible for marking a contestant's time for each timed event. There must be at least two timers who agree on each contestant's time for calf roping, steer wrestling and barrel racing. The times also mark the eight seconds during the saddle or bareback bronc and bull riding events.

Tippy toe – a horse or bull that walks on its front legs when most of their weight is off the ground.

Toes out – the preferred style of holding the feet at a 90 degree angle to the animal to ensure proper positioning.

Trappy – a short, quick choppy stride. This condition is predisposed in horses with short straight pasterns and straight shoulders.

Trash – a bucking animal with no set pattern.

Tree – the wooden or metal frame of a saddle.

Trotter – a team roping steer that hangs back on the rope and trots with its hind feet rather than running.

Tucked up – thin, and cut up in the flank like a greyhound.

Twitch – a stick with a rope or chain on one end that is placed around the upper lip of a horse and then twisted to release endorphins that will relax a horse and allow him to be handled.

Tying up – painful spastic condition of the large rump muscle masses; can result in muscle damage and inflammation. Most often seen in horses that are exercised irregularly.

Undershot – protruding under jaw.

Union animal – an animal that bucks until the sound of the eight second whistle, then quits.

Ungelded – an uncastrated horse.

Unsound – a horse with health problems or lameness.

V.M.D. – Veterinary Medical Doctor.

Vice – an acquired habit that is annoying or may interfere with the horse's usefulness.

Walleyed – iris of the eye of a light color.

Warm-blooded – designating any horse or breed of horse with Arabian or eastern blood in its breeding.

Weanling – a weaned foal. Foals are usually weaned about six months of age.

Weaving – a stable vice in which the horse continually rocks from side to side, shifting his weight from one front let to the other, causing the neck and head to sway as well.

West Nile Virus – is transmitted by birds and mosquitoes and the symptoms include fever, muscle weakness and partial paralysis. Vaccinate annually/ semi annually.

White line – zone on the horse's hoof where the insensitive laminae meet the sensitive laminae and grow out to the sole of the foot.

Winding – a twisting of the striding leg around and in front of the supporting leg so as to resemble a tight rope walker. This is also called rope walking.

Wind puff – non painful swelling of the fetlock joint which generally resolves in 15 minutes of light work. Most common in older horses.

Withers – the slight ridge in the horse's backbone, just behind the mane. It is the highest point on the horse's spine and from where height is measured.

Wolf teeth – rudimentary teeth which occur in front of the front upper molar tooth on either side of the jaw. They are usually removed as they interfere with the placement of the bit and hurt the horse when the bit moves around.

Yearling – a male or female horse between one and two years of age.

Yield mare – a mare that did not produce a foal during the current season.

Image 4 is a cartoonish weatern hat with

A rodeo queen crown and is above the Irish blessing

Insert image 4

May the road rise up to meet you.
May the wind always be at your back.
May the sun shine warm upon your face,
And rains fall soft upon your fields, and
Until we meet again, may God hold you
In the palm of His hand.
An Irish blessing

HAPPY TRAILS

CPSIA information can be obtained
at www.ICGtesting.com
Printed in the USA
LVHW010858300920
667476LV00005B/381